The Black Archive

BATTLEFIELD

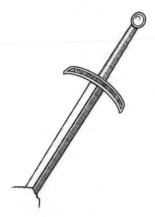

By Philip Purser-Hallard

Published August 2019 by Obverse Books

Cover Design © Cody Schell

Text © Philip Purser-Hallard, 2019

Range Editors: Paul Simpson, Philip Purser-Hallard

Philip would like to thank:

The staff at the BBC Written Archives Centre, especially Samantha Blake and Kate O'Brien, for their assistance and access to their files; Dave Owen, for access to his memory; and Jon Arnold, Stuart Douglas, Jim Cooray Smith and Paul Simpson for their support and encouragement.

To all the **New Adventures** authors, who kept the candle burning while Merlin was bound in the ice caves.

Also Available

CONTENTS

OVERVIEW

Serial Title: *Battlefield*

Writer: Ben Aaronovitch

Director: Michael Kerrigan

Original UK Transmission Dates: 6 September 1989 – 27 September 1989

Running Time: Episode 1: 24m 7s

Episode 2: 24m 8s

Episode 3: 24m 13s

Episode 4: 24m 15s

UK Viewing Figures: Episode 1: 3.1 million

Episode 2: 3.9 million

Episode 3: 3.6 million

Episode 4: 4.0 million

Regular Cast: Sylvester McCoy (The Doctor), Sophie Aldred (Ace)

Recurring Cast: Nicholas Courtney (Brigadier Lethbridge-Stewart)

Guest Cast: Jean Marsh (Morgaine), James Ellis (Peter Warmsly), Angela Bruce (Brigadier Winifred Bambera), Christopher Bowen (Mordred), Marcus Gilbert (Ancelyn), Angela Douglas (Doris), Noel Collins (Pat Rowlinson), June Bland (Elizabeth Rowlinson), Ling Tai (Shou Yuing), Robert Jezek (Sergeant Zbrigniev), Dorota Rae (Flight Lieutenant Lavel), Stefan Schwartz (Knight Commander), Paul Tomany (Major Husak), Marek Anton (The Destroyer)

Antagonists: Morgaine, Mordred, the Destroyer

Novelisation: *Doctor Who: Battlefield* by Marc Platt. **The Target Doctor Who Library** #152.

Responses:

'Battlefield is **awesome**. For a start, it's gorgeously shot on location. They actually used money on it [...] Also, it's a clever story [...] there's certainly a much larger epic tale going on here in between the scenes we actually see...'

[Tansy Rayner Roberts, '"She Vanquished Me": **Doctor Who** – *Battlefield*']

'[F]or all the excellent material [...] it's difficult to get past the terribly shaky opening few minutes of the show [...] and the utterly silly looking knights with their phoney, sparking gun blasts.'

[Andrew Cartmel, *Script Doctor: The Inside Story of Doctor Who 1986-89*, p159]

SYNOPSIS

Episode 1

An enigmatic signal summons **the Doctor** and **Ace** to England in Ace's near future. A military convoy escorting a nuclear missile is stranded next to Vortigern's Lake near Carbury, its electronics incapacitated by an electromagnetic pulse. This annoys both **Brigadier Winifred Bambera** of UNIT, who is in charge of the convoy, and **Peter Warmsly**, an archaeologist whose dig the vehicles are endangering. After visiting the site, an eighth-century battlefield, the Doctor and Ace check into the Gore Crow Hotel, owned by the blind **Elizabeth Rowlinson** and her husband **Pat**, where they meet **Shou Yuing**, a fellow customer. A scabbard from the dig is displayed on a wall.

Sergeant Zbrigniev apprises Bambera of the Doctor's history with UNIT, and the United Nations calls **Brigadier Lethbridge-Stewart** out of retirement to liaise with the Doctor. Over the protests of his wife **Doris**, Lethbridge-Stewart leaves for a briefing in London.

In woods near the hotel, a medieval-looking knight and **men-at-arms** who have fallen from the sky shoot one another with futuristic weapons. The knight, heavily outnumbered, is blown into the air by a grenade, landing in the hotel's brewery outhouse. The Doctor, Ace and Shou Yuing find the injured knight, **Ancelyn**, who speaks of 'Excalibur's call' and the return of King Arthur, and apparently recognises the Doctor as Merlin. Bambera arrives and threatens everyone, as do Ancelyn's enemies, led by **Mordred**.

Episode 2

The Doctor pretends to be Merlin and intimidates Mordred into withdrawing. Bambera overpowers Ancelyn, much to his delight. At a nearby ruin, Mordred and his men establish a gateway between 'two realities', causing earth tremors and the sudden violent flight of the scabbard across the hotel bar. Mordred's mother, the immortal **Morgaine**, arrives through the bridgehead. Despite the distance between them she magically addresses the Doctor, who she too calls 'Merlin', warning him not to interfere with her plans.

Lethbridge-Stewart and his pilot **Lavel** arrive from London by helicopter, but are brought down by Morgaine's sorcery. Lavel is injured in the crash and Lethbridge-Stewart goes to find help. Morgaine finds a war memorial, and scolds Mordred for not having held a ceremony to honour the dead. Lethbridge-Stewart finds them about to do so, and agrees to attend.

At the dig, the Doctor and Ace find an engraved message from the Doctor himself, pinpointing what turns out – after Ace blows it open with explosive – to be the entrance to a tunnel. They enter a spaceship under the lake, where they find **King Arthur** lying, apparently in suspended animation, next to his sword Excalibur – the source of the summoning signal and of the electromagnetic pulse. The Doctor explains that the spaceship, Ancelyn, Morgaine and Mordred come from another universe where the historical Arthur was closer to the myth. Ace pulls Excalibur from its housing, which activates a hostile security system. Ace escapes into an airlock, which fills with lake-water as the Doctor is knocked unconscious.

Episode 3

Ace emerges from the lake's surface, brandishing Excalibur, to the amazement of Warmsly, Ancelyn and Bambera. Lethbridge-Stewart and Shou Yuing arrive in the latter's car, and Lethbridge-Stewart descends to rescue the Doctor from the spaceship.

Bitter at his mother's scolding, Mordred goes to the hotel and drinks five pints of beer. The injured Lavel finds him, but so does Morgaine, who extracts strategic information from the pilot's brain, killing her in the process. She incinerates the body and pays for her son's drinks by restoring Elizabeth's sight.

The Doctor's party are attacked by Morgaine's men-at-arms on the way back to the hotel. Bambera and Ancelyn are separated from the others, and bond over their adversity. The others find UNIT troops under **Major Husak** taking charge of the hotel. They evacuate the Rowlinsons and Warmsly, though Shou Yuing avoids being taken away. At the Doctor's suggestion, Lethbridge-Stewart requisitions some silver bullets from Husak's quartermaster. The troops have also brought **Bessie**, the Doctor's modified vintage car. Lethbridge-Stewart and the Doctor go to check on the safety of the convoy. They arrive to find a battle in progress between UNIT and Morgaine's men, which the Doctor halts by yelling at them to stop.

Morgaine hopes to acquire Excalibur, which the Doctor has left with Ace and Shou Yuing, protected by a magical chalk circle. Morgaine attempts tries various forms of psychological attack then reveals her ultimate weapon, a chained demon called **the Destroyer**.

Episode 4

Again Morgaine communicates at a distance with the Doctor. Lethbridge-Stewart threatens Mordred, demanding Morgaine call off the Destroyer, but she refuses, giving up her son for dead. The Doctor and Lethbridge-Stewart arrive at the hotel and find it partially collapsed. Ace and Shou Yuing are alive, but Morgaine has vanished with the Destroyer and Excalibur. However, the Destroyer has left their magical passage open, so that the Doctor, Lethbridge-Stewart and Ace can follow them to the ruined castle. To defeat them Morgaine is forced to unchain the Destroyer, as he intended. As he prepares to devour the Earth, she is distracted by Mordred, who accuses her of betraying him, and the Doctor retrieves Excalibur before mother and son vanish. Lethbridge-Stewart kills the demon with the silver bullets, narrowly escaping with his life.

Back at the spaceship in the aftermath of the battle, they replace Excalibur, but Arthur does not awaken. Instead they learn, via a note left by the future Doctor known as Merlin, that Arthur has been dead since his final battle – and that Morgaine has just taken control of the missile from Bambera. Believing Bambera is dead, Ancelyn attacks Mordred ferociously. The Doctor tells Morgaine of the horrors of the nuclear war she intends to trigger, appealing to her sense of honour. She aborts the countdown, but demands that Arthur face her in single combat. The Doctor reveals that the king is dead, and Morgaine, who loved him, gives up her plans in grief.

Bambera arrests Morgaine and Mordred, and Ace blows up King Arthur's spaceship. Later they leave the Lethbridge-Stewarts' house with Shou Yuing, Doris and Bessie for a celebratory girls' night out, leaving Alistair, Ancelyn and the Doctor to do the housework.

INTRODUCTION

The 1989 season of **Doctor Who**, the last full season to be broadcast during the 20th century, is widely regarded as one of its creative peaks: the point where Andrew Cartmel hit his stride as Script Editor and prompted his scriptwriters to deliver a consistent run of stories whose emotional maturity, political engagement and thematic complexity showcased the true potential of **Doctor Who** as a sophisticated science-fiction drama, immediately before the BBC placed the series on indefinite hiatus.

Of these stories, *Ghost Light* is a fascinatingly labyrinthine meditation on change, difference and social mobility, whose setting, distilled from Victorian science, fiction and politics, is as allusive as its meaning is elusive. *The Curse of Fenric* is a postmodernist take on Norse mythology and vampire legend, in which predestination is the enemy and the faith of a Red Army zealot a surer safeguard against evil than that of an honest but troubled priest. And *Survival* is an award-winning playwright's interrogation of Thatcherism, using the seductive savagery of the animal kingdom as an extended metaphor, with an unusually nuanced characterisation of the Master and a lesbian subtext.

All three of these stories are excellent, and have been rightly praised by posterity. This book is not about any of them.

The first serial broadcast in that 1989 run, preceding these three, was *Battlefield*, a blending of **Doctor Who** continuity with Arthurian myth that posterity has regarded less favourably. For many years (until *The Lie of the Land* took the crown in 2017) it held the record for the lowest viewing figures the series had ever received. This cannot reasonably be seen as a reflection of the story's quality, as the lowest figures were garnered by the first episode and could not therefore have been based on the viewers' impressions of the story; in fact, the last episode was watched by nearly a million more people than the first.

Nevertheless, the impression has persisted that this lack of popularity was deserved. Such consensus as has grown up among those who consider it worthwhile to hold opinions about old **Doctor Who** stories tells us that *Battlefield* is confusing and ends anticlimactically; that the action sequences in particular are poorly directed; and that it looks cheap and unintentionally comedic – perhaps even like a children's programme[1]. Some have more particular criticisms: that the story's identification of the Doctor with Merlin is 'laboured', or at least 'less subtle' than mythic allusions in other stories[2]; that its attempts at feminism fail[3]; that Brigadier Bambera repeatedly says 'shame' when she obviously means 'shit'[4]; and that the demonic Destroyer spends too little

---

[1] Listing examples of all these opinions would be excessive: variants on them can be found in most of the available **Doctor Who** episode guides.

[2] Newman, Kim, *BFI TV Classics: Doctor Who* p16; Rafer, David, 'Mythic Identity in **Doctor Who**' p133, in Butler, David, ed, *Time and Relative Dissertations in Space: Critical Perspectives on Doctor Who*.

[3] McCormack, Una, 'No Competition', p36, in Stanish, Deborah, and LM Myles, eds, *Chicks Unravel Time: Women Journey through Every Season of Doctor Who*.

[4] Wood, Tat, *About Time 6: The Unauthorised Guide to Doctor Who – 1985-1989 – Seasons 22 to 26, The TV Movie* p291.

time onscreen[5]. The only widely praised aspects are the Destroyer's design and the characterisation and performance of Morgaine.

That the story turned out this way is surprising. The script is, after all, the work of Ben Aaronovitch, the writer of the previous year's widely-revered *Remembrance of the Daleks* (1988), which stands with *Ghost Light*, *The Curse of Fenric* and *Survival* in terms of quality. Aaronovitch would go on to write some of the most highly-regarded of Virgin Publishing's original **Doctor Who** novels, **The New Adventures**, and has since become a bestselling genre novelist with his series of urban fantasy police procedurals beginning with *Rivers of London* (2011). Though *Battlefield* is an early work, much of Aaronovitch's success throughout his career has been based on reimagining pre-existing narrative elements in new and interesting ways, from the Daleks of *Remembrance* to the London history and folklore of the **Rivers of London** books[6]. The story's concept, pitting high-tech knights from an alternative dimension against near-future soldiers from the mundane world, was certainly ambitious, but no more so than a war between Dalek factions in a faithful recreation of 1960s London, which *Remembrance* had pulled off with aplomb.

Battlefield's director, Michael Kerrigan, already had a successful career in children's TV, and would go on to direct episodes of **The Bill** (1984-2010), **Coronation Street** (1960-) and, in 2008, **The Sarah Jane Adventures** (2007-11). Particularly relevant to *Battlefield* was

---

[5] Campbell, Mark, *The Pocket Essential: Doctor Who* p84.
[6] His **New Adventures** *Transit* (1992) and *The Also People* (1995) likewise draw heavily on the cyberpunk futures of William Gibson and the utopian space operas of Iain M Banks respectively.

15

his work on **Knights of God** (1987), a young adult serial set in a dystopian future Britain with prominent Arthurian overtones.

The cast would (with the possible exception of Ling Tai, known primarily as a children's TV presenter) have seemed equally reassuring. Two actors associated with **Doctor Who** since the 1960s reappeared, one of them (Nicholas Courtney) reprising the character he had played intermittently since 1968, the other (Jean Marsh) the winner of an Emmy Award for her acting in **Upstairs, Downstairs** (1971-75, 2010-12), a series which she co-created. Other cast members had been involved in **Z-Cars** (1962-78) (James Ellis), **Angels** (1975-83) (Angela Bruce) and the **Carry On** films (1958-78) (Angela Douglas).

Finally, of course, four of *Battlefield*'s key personnel – Sylvester McCoy and Sophie Aldred, Andrew Cartmel and Producer John Nathan-Turner – were exactly those who had already delivered the outstanding *Remembrance* (and its only somewhat less respected 1988 peers *The Happiness Patrol* and *The Greatest Show in the Galaxy*), and would go on to create *Ghost Light*, *The Curse of Fenric* and *Survival*. All the elements were in place for *Battlefield* to become as excellent a story as any of its 1989 stablemates.

Evidently, this did not happen.

This book is not an attempt to rehabilitate *Battlefield*. Though a few of the criticisms mentioned above are unnecessarily harsh, nearly all are to some extent justified. Nevertheless, despite the story's various missteps and mishaps, it succeeds in certain important respects, and it is this tension in which this book is most interested.

Because, in the terms in which I have praised those other stories of the 1989 season – for their emotional maturity, political engagement and thematic complexity – *Battlefield* is better able to compete with its peers than the common view of it would allow. If it cannot reasonably be called a success by the standards of late-1980s **Doctor Who**, neither is it wholly a failure. The gap between these two options is sufficient to comfortably accommodate a story which, though flawed, is intelligent, literate, evocative, occasionally lyrical, and even – at times when it particularly needs to be – subtle.

CHAPTER 1: 'ONE PAINSTAKING LAYER AT A TIME'

It will help to understand some of *Battlefield*'s particular structural issues if I outline, as far as possible, how the story evolved from the author's earliest ideas to the broadcast version (and somewhat beyond).

According to **Doctor Who** historian Andrew Pixley, Ben Aaronovitch first proposed an Arthurian story to Andrew Cartmel during the summer of 1987[7]. A three-episode version was developed as far as a single script and two episode synopses, but was placed on hold when Cartmel commissioned Aaronovitch to write *Remembrance of the Daleks*.

Pixley's article gives few details of this earliest iteration of the story that would become *Battlefield*. The three episodes were to have no studio scenes (which is not true of *Battlefield* as broadcast), and Aaronovitch 'wanted to give scientific explanations to numerous elements of [Arthurian] mythology' – also not an aspect that comes through strongly in the transmitted story. Perhaps most notably, despite a considerable military presence in the plot, the story did not involve UNIT or Brigadier Lethbridge-Stewart. Nevertheless, the basic concept ('an epic military battle with knights from space') was

---

[7] Pixley, Andrew, 'The DWM Archive: *Battlefield*', *Doctor Who Magazine* (DWM) #317, p27. (An abridged version of this article appears in *Doctor Who: The Complete History* volume 45.) Despite its obvious appositeness, 'Knight Fall' seems not to have been a working title for *Battlefield*, but attached to an earlier, unrelated pitch from Aaronovitch (Cartmel, Andrew, *Script Doctor: The Inside Story of Doctor Who 1986-89*, p89).

clearly in place, as were the characters who would become Shou Yuing and Brigadier Bambera[8].

First Story Treatment

The earliest story treatment that still exists in the BBC's Written Archives Centre at Caversham is a four-episode synopsis dated 12 September 1988 and entitled 'Storm over Avallion'[9]. The extra episode has allowed the material to become a UNIT story, featuring the retired Lethbridge-Stewart and set in '1999'[10]. The treatment follows the outline of the broadcast story reasonably closely for the first two episodes: though there are numerous differences of detail involving scene settings, character identities and their functions and movements, all the major story beats are present.

In episode 3, the story begins to diverge from the shape it would eventually take. The cliffhanger resolution involves the Doctor trapping the Guardians of the spaceship (described as 'ethereal snakes') in a container, after somehow turning their own strength against them. Later, the Shou Yuing character (called 'Thai' in this version[11]) is left in sole charge of Excalibur while Ace is with the Doctor and Lethbridge-Stewart. While the Doctor fights off an

---

[8] Pixley, 'The DWM Archive: *Battlefield*', p27.

[9] BBC Written Archives Centre (WAC) file T65/271/1, story treatment dated 12 September 1988.

[10] 'When it became a four-parter there was suddenly room to put UNIT in' (Aaronovitch, quoted in Cartmel, *Script Doctor*, p153).

[11] The unusual name makes one wonder whether Ling Tai – a former regular on the BBC children's show **Crackerjack!** (1955-84) who had also been an extra in *The Leisure Hive* (1980) and *Warriors of the Deep* (1984) – had already been approached to appear in the story at this stage.

incursion into the ship by Mordred and some of his knights, Lethbridge-Stewart and Ace rescue Thai, using technology that disrupts the 'control systems' of Morgaine's armour. As Morgaine leaves, however, she pulls out some of Ace's hair, which she later uses in the summoning ritual for her Demon. The Demon requires a willing sacrifice, and through a form of voodoo-like mind-control Morgaine will be able to compel Ace to fulfil this role[12]. The Doctor arrives in time to save Ace from killing herself, but the Demon has already manifested, and it still demands a willing sacrifice, or it will destroy all life on Earth. This suits Morgaine's purposes equally well, as her magical bridge can only operate while living beings exist on both worlds: with life extinguished on Earth the sleeping king – here called 'A'tur' – will be trapped there for eternity.

Episode 4 of this draft is very different from the familiar version: it begins with Lethbridge-Stewart's death in combat with the Demon. Dismissing his subordinate, Major McKinnawe, and the Czechoslovakian UNIT troops, he calls in a rocket strike which he believes will destroy it and himself. The rockets hit the site and kill Lethbridge-Stewart, but it is the Brigadier's willing sacrifice of his own life, rather than the missiles, which satisfies the Demon and banishes it back to its home dimension. Morgaine then attacks the missile convoy, intending (in explicit violation of the 'codes of Chivalry') to provoke a nuclear war – again with the specific aim of causing the extinction of life on Earth. Bambera initially resists Morgaine's attempts to learn the launch codes from her and is struck down in punishment by Mordred; as in the broadcast story,

---

[12] This would appear to stretch the definition of 'willing' considerably, which is perhaps why this plot point was changed.

Ancelyn sees her apparently dead and retaliates, and is nearly killed for his pains – until, in this version, a reviving Bambera intervenes and shoots Mordred dead. The Doctor confronts Morgaine, releasing the Guardians he trapped aboard the spaceship to attack her. Meanwhile, Ace swims down to the spaceship and replaces Excalibur in its socket, restoring A'tur to life.

With the power of Excalibur the revived king is able to 'neutralise' the missile, and then restores Mordred to life in return for Morgaine's pledge of eternal allegiance. Ancelyn and Bambera, intending to marry, return to Ancelyn's dimension with A'tur, Morgaine and Mordred. The Doctor mourns Lethbridge-Stewart, apparently considering giving up his travels, but instead electing to continue them in his memory[13].

Although the treatment ends with a note from Aaronovitch apologising that episode 4 and the end of episode 3 are 'not completed [...] very rough', this storyline is in several respects more coherent than what was eventually broadcast. Notably, Morgaine has a clear motivation for wanting to instigate nuclear war: with life on Earth eradicated, A'tur will be unable to trouble her in her own dimension. (In the broadcast version, this interesting idea survives only in Mordred's far-from-explicit line 'Across the abyss life calls to life, biomass to biomass, energy to energy.'[14]) The Doctor, Ace and the Ancelyn-Bambera duo all have clear and distinct roles at the story's climax, and the Doctor wins by dint of a clever plan rather than by talking Morgaine out of her intentions. Lethbridge-

---

[13] BBC WAC file T65/271/1, 12 September 1988.
[14] *Battlefield* episode 2.

Stewart's self-sacrifice gives him a clear and vitally important role in the story. The Doctor is unusually given an emotional arc, ending on a melancholy note reminiscent of *Remembrance of the Daleks*, but for the Doctor – and presumably for many of the intended audience, who would remember Lethbridge-Stewart from his previous appearances – a more personal one.

Second Story Treatment

The second treatment is dated just over a week later, 20 September 1988. It still uses the title 'Storm over Avallion'. Winifred Bambera, who in the prior treatment was a US Air Force Captain, has become a Brigadier working for UNIT. Lavender Warmington, a Carbury trustee, has changed gender and become Peter Warmsly. Major McKinnawe is still present, but Sgt Zbrigniev, Major 'Hasek' and 'Captain' Richards (who appears, as Lieutenant Richards, only briefly as a radio voice in the broadcast version) appear for the first time. Thai has been given the name Shou Yuing, and Lethbridge-Stewart is a General. Rather than the specific date of '1999', the story is set 'in the near future'.

An early footnote gives a recent biography of Lethbridge-Stewart, maintaining continuity with *Mawdryn Undead* (1983) in having him originally retire in the mid-1970s. It mentions what sound like the Dalek and Cybermen incursions seen in *Resurrection of the Daleks* (1984) and *The Tenth Planet* (1966, but set in 1986) and suggests that UNIT's remit was expanded following 'the Moscow Summit in 1987'[15]. General Lethbridge-Stewart was recalled to command its

---

[15] There was a real summit between US and Soviet leaders in 1987, but it took place in Washington; a Moscow summit followed in 1988. This could be absent-mindedness about recent events on

'Extra-Terrestrial Threat Section': though he is first seen gardening, this is because it is his day off rather than because he is still retired.

For much of the first three episodes the story is very similar, and the two synopses are sometimes identical word for word. There are a few significant differences, however. Dr Brown, an archaeologist excavating the Vortigern's Lake site (and a sceptic about the Arthurian legends, an element which is not carried over to the TV story), is now annihilated when Morgaine takes the knowledge of Excalibur from his mind, rather than surviving it. Mordred has cold feet, doubting the justification for his mother's war and even protesting Brown's death – but is told by his mother that the ethics of war 'no longer apply'. A second footnote promises a 'pseudoscientific explanation' of the hold Ace's hair gives Morgaine over her, involving genetics and psionics.

Episode 4 makes significantly different choices. The Demon is now a 'Death Elemental', more directly capable of extinguishing life on Earth. Lethbridge-Stewart no longer dies in the rocket strike, but survives to fight the zombie army the Elemental raises from Morgaine's fallen men-at-arms. Instead of deliberately sacrificing himself, Lethbridge-Stewart dies from the 'energy feedback' when he impales the Elemental with Excalibur. Later, the Doctor engages Morgaine in a direct battle of wills before distracting her by unleashing the Guardians. He then anticlimactically disarms the nuclear missile by pulling its plug and cutting off its power. A'tur returns as before and takes Morgaine and Mordred prisoner, but at the Doctor's urging agrees to rehabilitate rather than execute

---

Aaronovitch's part, rather than a considered attempt to create an alternative history of the Cold War.

them, ending the conflict between them. Ancelyn begs A'tur's leave to marry Bambera, which surprises her. As the spaceship leaves, though, the Doctor implies that she and Ancelyn were fated to fall in love, as 'Ancelyn' is a form of the name 'Lancelot', and 'Winifred' a modern version of 'Guinevere'[16]. This thought seems to cheer him from his melancholy following Lethbridge-Stewart's death[17].

In the first treatment A'tur acted as a deus ex machina in the plot – a powerful yet arbitrary presence which manifests itself at the end of a story to resolve matters to the author's, and hopefully the audience's, satisfaction. In this second version Mordred is not killed, so does not require resurrection, and the threat of the missile is dealt with – albeit with comic bathos – by the Doctor. A'tur is thus seen to be less godlike in his powers, and the Doctor in his Merlin persona is given a stronger role in manipulating him. Lethbridge-Stewart's death is more arbitrary, however: though the Doctor has warned him that there is 'a drawback' to using Excalibur on the Elemental, there is no obvious reason for this plot device except that his death is thematically required. In other respects – apart perhaps from the zombies, which are a slightly febrile touch – this version retains the strengths of the previous treatment.

---

[16] Neither of which is true, although Aaronovitch had a source which was confusing on the point; see Chapter 4. Judging by her callsign 'Seabird' (and especially Major Husak's observation in episode 3 that 'The Seabirds are still operational'), Bambera's surname is a misspelling of the West African ethnonym adopted by the African-American intellectual Toni Cade Bambara, the author of the short story collection *The Sea Birds Are Still Alive* (1977).

[17] BBC WAC T65/271/1, story treatment dated 20 September 1988.

One further point of interest is that both treatments explicitly call Morgaine and Mordred's faction the 'S'rax', a name that in the broadcast story survives only as part of a title claimed by Morgaine in episode 2. In the transmitted version Ancelyn's people are 'the Britons' – the Celtic people of Britain to whom Arthur is traditionally understood to have belonged; or rather, presumably, their alternative-world equivalents – but here they are 'Br'tons'. This suggests that 'S'rax' is a transformation of 'Saxons', the invading enemies against whom the Britons are pitted in many versions of the Arthurian myths.

Rehearsal Script

The final full version of the story in the Caversham archive is the rehearsal script, now retitled *Battlefield*[18], although episode 1 still bears the title 'Storm over Avallion'[19]. In that first episode Ancelyn still refers to 'A'tur' and the 'Br'tons', but the later uses of these names are normalised (as they all would be onscreen) to 'Arthur' and 'Britons'. The plot follows the form of the broadcast story. Dr Brown has been eliminated and his plot functions distributed between Warmsly and Flt Lt Lavel, who is given an equivalent to Brown's death scene. Lethbridge-Stewart is demoted to Brigadier again, and is once more seen to be brought out of retirement. His UNIT VTOL jet is now (more practically from an effects point of view) a helicopter, and is no longer brought down by systems failure as Mordred opens the gateway between worlds, but by a

---

[18] It went through an interim stage of being called 'The Battlefield', according to Pixley ('The DWM Archive: *Battlefield*' p30).
[19] BBC WAC T65/271/1, rehearsal script (undated). Readthroughs of the script began on 28 April 1989.

direct magical attack from Morgaine. The third Doctor's car Bessie is added to the elements being brought back from the series' past. Rather than being controlled by Morgaine, Ace is with Shou Yuing as the sorceress attempts to take Excalibur from her, giving Morgaine the opportunity to pit them against each other. The idea that the Destroyer first appears in human form before revealing his true shape is introduced (only to be abandoned before filming).

Episode 4 sees the most radical changes from the previous versions, with Lethbridge-Stewart surviving but Arthur revealed to be dead. The zombies are absent, the Brigadier now kills the Destroyer with silver bullets and lives to tell the tale (though he is briefly mistaken for dead by the Doctor), and Ace's attempt to revive the king – now made with Lethbridge-Stewart, Ancelyn and the Doctor in attendance – fails, instead uncovering the note from the Doctor's future self. Rather than using the trapped Guardians, which in this iteration have been deactivated, the Doctor simply confronts Morgaine and distracts her with the news that Arthur is dead, allowing him to abort the countdown. Ancelyn and Mordred still fight after Ancelyn believes Mordred has killed Bambera, but it is the Doctor rather than Bambera herself who rescues Ancelyn. The coda at Lethbridge-Stewart's house is added[20].

Though some events survive in very broad outline from the story treatments – Lethbridge-Stewart kills the demon, Morgaine captures the missile by force and tries to fire it, but the Doctor prevents her – the version of *Battlefield* episode 4 seen in the rehearsal scripts is thus radically changed. These alterations have the effect of making the ending messier, as Ace and Lethbridge-

---

[20] BBC WAC T65/271/1, rehearsal script.

Stewart – who previously spent the climax, respectively, reviving A'tur and dead – are left blowing up the spaceship for no terribly compelling reason while the Doctor confronts Morgaine alone. In place of the final scene of Ancelyn and Bambera leaving with A'tur in the spaceship while the Doctor mourns Lethbridge-Stewart, we are left with an ending of incongruously cosy domestic comedy which feels as if it belongs to a different story altogether, perhaps even a different series.

Aaronovitch's decision not to have the living Arthur appear onscreen is almost certainly a sensible one. The second treatment had already reduced A'tur's involvement in resolving the plot, and removing him altogether allows for an ending where the protagonist and his allies overcome the antagonists without external aid. **Doctor Who** has always been suspicious of higher powers, and in the stories surrounding *Battlefield*, the Gods of Ragnarok, Light and Fenric are all villains, not supernatural allies of the heroes. The series also has a tradition of scepticism towards worldly authority – not least in the original UNIT era, as seen in stories such as *The Claws of Axos* (1971) and *The Sea Devils* (1972) – and during the late 1980s this became sharply politicised. Telling us that the Doctor will become Merlin is a revelation in keeping with what we know of the character's own wisdom and power, but to show him actively endorsing a supernaturally-appointed monarch would have been distinctly off-message for the period.

An unfortunate knock-on effect, however, is that in Arthur's absence there is no authority which can sensibly be trusted to take Morgaine and Mordred into custody. This has led to a plot hole whose absurdity many reviewers have remarked on: the assumption that UNIT can successfully keep a dimension-hopping sorceress prisoner[21].

The decision not to kill off Lethbridge-Stewart is more awkward still. According to Pixley, it was made at the prompting of Cartmel and John Nathan-Turner, **Doctor Who**'s Producer since 1980; ironically, Courtney himself had been keen to be given a death scene[22]. Nathan-Turner believed it would be lost in a script already full of incident, while Cartmel simply felt it was gratuitous[23], writing in 2005 that 'I've far too much affection for the character, and for Nick [Courtney], to be the one responsible for putting an end to the Brigadier.'[24] Both men normally had sound storytelling instincts, but in this instance Lethbridge-Stewart's survival collapses the shape of a story to which his death would have been the capstone, creating an emotional and thematic void in episode 4 that Aaronovitch's new ending fails to fill. Quite aside from his supplantation by Bambera and her 1990s iteration of UNIT, much of Lethbridge-Stewart's involvement in *Battlefield* acts as a foreshadowing of his death: his planting of a tree (in the rehearsal script he wonders how high it will grow); Doris's concern and his

---

[21] See, among others, Wood, *About Time 6*, p301. Wood suggests, not unreasonably, that Morgaine's sense of honour might prohibit her from making an escape if she is honestly repentant for her crimes; I would add that the fact that UNIT uses silver bullets suggests that they might be more prepared for supernatural prisoners than reviewers give them credit for. However, with neither of these possibilities mentioned onscreen, the point stands.
[22] Pixley, 'The DWM Archive: *Battlefield*' p29
[23] Pixley, 'The DWM Archive: *Battlefield*' p30.
[24] Cartmel, *Script Doctor*, p155.

own initial reluctance at his being pulled out of retirement[25]; his participation in the ceremony to honour the war dead[26]; his insistence that 'UNIT looks after its own, alive or dead'[27]. The Doctor's lines after Lethbridge-Stewart's apparent death would also work far better if not immediately undercut by his return to consciousness[28].

While one can imagine that Cartmel and Nathan-Turner may have had an eye on extraneous considerations, such as the possibility of reusing Lethbridge-Stewart again in a future series[29], or the potentially hostile reaction of fans to his death, it is difficult to argue that *Battlefield* as a self-contained story would not be improved by following through on this promise. A version in which Lethbridge-Stewart's mutually fatal showdown with the Destroyer was delayed still further, to form a simultaneous climax with the Doctor's confrontation with Morgaine, would do much to mend the structural issues I have noted. It would allow the Destroyer more screen time, emphasise the thematic parallel between the demon and the nuclear warhead, and create a resonance between Morgaine's mourning for Arthur and the Doctor's for Lethbridge-Stewart. And a heroic death scene would have been a much more fitting send-off for the character than his eventual return in **The**

---

[25] Episode 1.

[26] Episode 2.

[27] This line from the script for episode 3 was cut from the broadcast version, but survives in the Special Edition. (The Special Edition is a single feature-length presentation, not organised into episodes.)

[28] Episode 4.

[29] Though there is no evidence of any concrete plans to do so – see Chapter 2.

Sarah Jane Adventures: *Enemy of the Bane* (2008), where Courtney is depressingly ill-looking and frail, and plays little part in the action.

Though a small point in comparison, the excision of the Doctor's capture of the spaceship's Guardians to use later as a weapon against Morgaine is another loss. It deprives the story, and the character, of a minor piece of cleverness which there seems no obvious reason not to have retained, except perhaps that the 'malign being imprisoned in a container' plot device is also used in *The Curse of Fenric*[30].

Broadcast Version

Some final changes to the script were made before filming. These include the loss of some lines in episode 1 where Ace attempts to establish exactly what the year is, and some in episode 2 where the Doctor still states that Ancelyn is a 'variation' on Lancelot – and interestingly, before explaining that the other world's Arthur is 'closer to the myth', mentions having met the real Arthur from Ace's history, a minor Dark Ages warlord. James Ellis added several quotations from Tennyson to his lines as Peter Warmsly[31]. A scene with Doris listening to the radio news, which would have sketched out a little more of the future world's current affairs, was cut from episode 4.

---

[30] The zombie men-at-arms, if used, might also have seemed uncomfortably reminiscent of that story's undead monsters.
[31] Pixley, 'The DWM Archive: *Battlefield*' p28; Cartmel, *Script Doctor* p152.

Most significantly, the final confrontation between the Doctor and Morgaine was entirely rewritten – a last-minute amendment by Cartmel, though made at Aaronovitch's behest[32]. As already noted, Morgaine's original motivation was to destroy Earth's biosphere and thus prevent Arthur from returning home. In the rehearsal script, her motivation has become flimsier: her only purpose is to destroy Arthur, and she is glad to die herself knowing that he will die with her. Similarly, in the absence from the rehearsal script of the trapped Guardians, the showdown becomes less dramatic: the Doctor merely reveals that Arthur is already dead, shocking Morgaine sufficiently for him to abort the countdown. He then tells her she should have found herself a worthier cause[33]. Aaronovitch was right to think that the scene as presented in the rehearsal script would have come across as a disappointing anticlimax.

(It is noticeable that this original resolution – the villain discovering, after a timespan measured in millennia, that the object of their intended revenge is dead, and losing their motivation as a result – is broadly the same as that of *Dragonfire* (1987), also script-edited by Cartmel, though the effect on *Dragonfire*'s Kane is more catastrophic than on Morgaine. Kane, who unlike Arthur actually uses suspended animation technology, is, like Morgaine, a villain capable of romantic love, although he is well aware that his beloved Xana has been dead for 3,000 years. It is conceivable that some of these similarities informed Cartmel's revision of Aaronovitch's resolution.)

---

[32] Pixley, 'The DWM Archive: *Battlefield*' pp33-34; Cartmel, *Script Doctor* p158.
[33] BBC WAC T65/271/1, rehearsal script.

Though they had to be cut down considerably in post-production editing, Cartmel's rewrites effectively create the scene as broadcast[34]. The Doctor's eloquent obloquy against nuclear war is his, as are Morgaine's emotional memories of Arthur as her lover[35]. Although this was a very late change, taking place after many of Morgaine's scenes had already been filmed, the revelation that she loves Arthur, and has in fact been hoping that he would be revived so she could see him again, both deepens and alters her character. It does, however, leave her with even less reason for wanting to trigger a nuclear holocaust on Earth, and this remains a glaring plot hole in *Battlefield* as broadcast. (Perhaps the best explanation available is that Morgaine was hoping all along that Merlin would talk her out of it – giving her the opportunity to demand, as she does, to face the awakened Arthur in single combat.)

One final difference between the rehearsal script and the transmitted *Battlefield* is not a change to the script so much as a decision to completely ignore a key element of it. In terms of what makes it to the screen, this was arguably the single most disastrous decision made during the story's development. Both story treatments are clear that the knights and Morgaine wear a form of high-tech powered armour, and that Morgaine in particular looks like a 'golden robot' in hers. Her armour's control systems are a minor plot point in the first treatment[36]. The rehearsal script goes into more detail: Ancelyn's armour, which has shielding to protect him during re-entry to the atmosphere, is said to be black, embossed with swirling designs, with a mirrored faceplate;

---

[34] Cartmel, *Script Doctor* pp158-59.
[35] BBC WAC T65/271/1, studio script changes dated 11 May 1989.
[36] BBC WAC T65/271/1, 12 and 20 September 1988.

Morgaine's troops wear a grey-blue gunmetal variant, with similar designs 'but a touch more barbaric'. When Ace asks, 'Is it an android?' she is responding to how Ancelyn's armour makes him look, and rather than merely replying 'No, it's a human,' the Doctor specifies that 'it's a human in powered armour.'[37] The point made by these descriptions is that the knights represent a civilisation whose superficial medieval stylings disguise alien technology at an advanced level.

As is immediately obvious to anybody watching *Battlefield*, this aesthetic is not that of the story as made. As Pixley reports, Michael Kerrigan and costume designer Anushia Nieradzik 'used stock armour with a few minimal changes for the knights, ignoring Aaronovitch's idea of a futuristic alien combat suit.'[38] (Morgaine's somewhat feminised armour in gold and bronze is more visually impressive, but gives a similar impression of antiquity.) Aaronovitch believes that, rather than stock armour, 'They made it especially. They **especially made** the wrong kind of armour.'[39] While using stock armour would have been the least expensive option, conventional armour would still have been cheaper to design and make – especially given its potential to become stock armour for future BBC productions – than Aaronovitch's cybernetic battle-suits, so the decision represents a budget saving whichever option was taken.

It is only a slight exaggeration to say that this costuming choice transforms *Battlefield* from a high-concept fable in which the

---

[37] BBC WAC T65/271/1, rehearsal script.
[38] Pixley, 'The DWM Archive: *Battlefield*' p32.
[39] Cartmel, *Script Doctor* p151.

Arthurian myths are reinterpreted in futuristic SF terms into a Pythonesque travesty where men in battered medieval ironmongery fly through the air with no visible means of support, in one short-sighted, budget-saving stroke. To be fair to Kerrigan and Nieradzik, it may be that Aaronovitch's central premise was in fact unfilmable on a BBC budget, but in that case it is surprising that Cartmel and Nathan-Turner allowed him to develop it so far.

Later Evolution

Some elements were filmed but cut from the broadcast version, and were later restored in the 'Special Edition' included on the 2008 BBC DVD release. These include some lines from Lavel briefing Lethbridge-Stewart on UNIT's activities elsewhere, and incidentally sketching in some of the geopolitical background of Aaronovitch's 1990s; the Doctor explaining to Ace that Arthur's spaceship is bioengineered, and mentioning 'Clarke's Law' ('Any advanced form of technology is indistinguishable from magic') and its corollary ('Any advanced form of magic is indistinguishable from technology')[40]; a recurring motif in which Lethbridge-Stewart patronises Ace as 'the latest one' of the Doctor's companions; a scene by Lavel's body in which Ace and Shou Yuing deduce that Excalibur forms part of the spaceship's control systems; and some of the material cut from the Doctor's showdown with Morgaine.

---

[40] In fact this is Clarke's **Third** Law, named after SF author Arthur C Clarke (the first two are not widely remembered). In its original form it reads 'Any sufficiently advanced form of technology is indistinguishable from magic' ('Clarke's Laws', *The Encyclopedia of Science Fiction*).

In a final stage of evolution, the story was novelised in 1991, not by Aaronovitch but by Marc Platt, the scriptwriter responsible for *Ghost Light* who would later, like Aaronovitch, write for Virgin's **New Adventures** novels, and continues to contribute to Big Finish Productions' 21st-century **Doctor Who** audio series. It is apparent that the novel is based on an amalgamation of different versions of the script: scenes from the rehearsal script such as Ace's attempt to find out from the Doctor what the year is and Doris listening to the radio news are reproduced in the book, as are the 'Clarke's Law' and 'latest one' scenes from the Special Edition; but Warmsly quotes Tennyson much as he does onscreen, and the Doctor's confrontation with Morgaine is Cartmel's rewritten version from the broadcast episode 4[41]. There is also a great deal of additional material, including detail of both Arthur's world and the near future (explicitly 1998-99 in the book), which in the absence of evidence to the contrary I assume to be Platt's elaboration upon Aaronovitch's worldbuilding rather than anything based closely on the latter's ideas for the story[42].

'A Precise and Delicate Skill'

The history of *Battlefield*'s development is something of a cautionary tale for scriptwriters and script editors. Among other

---

[41] Platt, Marc, *Battlefield* pp30, 156, 88, 103, 98, 166-68.

[42] Speaking subjectively, the additional scenes seem to have the gothic flavour of the worlds Platt created for his **New Adventures** *Cat's Cradle: Time's Crucible* (1992) and *Lungbarrow* (1997), rather than the cyberpunk futures of Aaronovitch's *Transit* and *The Also People*. Accordingly, although the novelisation frequently expands on matters which are unclear in the televised story, I will not be drawing directly on this material when analysing the latter.

lessons, it acts as a reminder that imagination will always be constrained by budget (though the success of *Remembrance* might have made the inexperienced Aaronovitch overconfident in this respect). It shows that bringing back a popular character may not be the tour de force one might hope for, unless those in charge are prepared for them to be subject to the same dramatic possibilities as any other guest character. Most of all perhaps, it demonstrates the importance of having a clear idea of how a story will end before starting to write it.

In Aaronovitch's favour, though, his willingness to make changes to his story is a laudable example of the flexibility often required of screenwriters. In hindsight, another script draft and some different decisions at production and costuming levels could potentially have fixed enough of *Battlefield*'s issues that it might now be remembered as a classic to match its 1989 contemporaries. In 1989, however, its makers were subject to the very real pressures of TV production schedules and budgets.

And so, instead of the archetypal platonic *Battlefield* that could have been, we are left with the one that was broadcast, and which we can only respond to on its own terms.

CHAPTER 2: DALEKS, MASTERPLANS
'A Philosophical Pair'

Like *Battlefield*, Aaronovitch's previous **Doctor Who** story, *Remembrance of the Daleks*, involves the encroachment into Britain, in a period well within the lifetime of many viewers, of a war between armoured soldiers belonging to factions of a far-flung civilisation, among whom the Doctor is a figure of legend. While one group comes in force, led by an ancient enemy of the Doctor and calling on the services of an individual that is a powerful weapon in its own right[43], the other side is outnumbered and forced to recruit local allies. There is a struggle for control of a legendary weapon that the Doctor may have had a hand in creating, after which the Doctor talks his remaining adversary into surrender. Several scenes take place in an establishment that serves drinks, and some in a churchyard.

Admittedly, the somewhat formulaic nature of **Doctor Who** plotting means that this parlour game can be played with many pairs of stories (the parallels between *Remembrance* and *Silver Nemesis* (1988), for instance, are also striking), and there are substantial differences between *Remembrance* and *Battlefield* even at a summary level – most obviously the fact that the Doctor becomes Ancelyn's ally while being antagonistic to both sides in the Dalek civil war.

---

[43] In Aaronovitch's novelisation, the Special Weapons Dalek is known to the other Imperial Daleks as 'the Abomination', a similarly portentous title to that of 'the Destroyer' (Aaronovitch, Ben, *Remembrance of the Daleks* (1990) p128).

The similarities between the stories go deeper than the storyline, however. Aaronovitch has said that *Battlefield*:

> '...couldn't be a story about the Doctor's past, because we were already doing that with *Remembrance of the Daleks*. So it had to be the Doctor's future – his **future** comes back to bite him in the arse. [...] This fitted nicely with the fact that it was set in the near future, just the way the Dalek story was set in the near past. I saw them as a pair, a philosophical pair, if that's not too pretentious a way of putting it.'[44]

This suggests that even the contrasts between the stories may be seen as thoughtful inversions. For instance, *Remembrance*'s central plot device is a coffin that turns out to be capable of travelling in space, spreading death on an interstellar scale, while *Battlefield* revolves around a spaceship that proves to be a tomb, burying Morgaine's universe-hopping ambitions. Similarly, the apparent paradox that the story set in the past involves aliens and spaceships, while the one about knights and sorcery is set in the future, may be explained by such a thematic opposition. *Remembrance* uses the Daleks, a longstanding symbol of Nazism, to examine the thuggery of racist groups prominent in the 1980s such as the National Front as a revival of Britain's own past fascist movement, while *Battlefield*'s Destroyer is an emblem of nuclear holocaust, a fear inevitably belonging to the near future. This perhaps also explains the contrast between urban and countryside settings, as resurgent racism in the 1980s was a predominantly inner-city phenomenon and the Daleks had been associated with

---

[44] Quoted in Cartmel, *Script Doctor*, p150.

cities since their first appearance; whereas both the quests of Arthurian knights and the futures of post-apocalyptic science fiction tend to be predominantly rural.

Admittedly, the point that the messages from the Doctor's future self in *Battlefield* are the equivalents of *Remembrance*'s relics of the past is somewhat obscured by the fact that *Battlefield* **also** draws heavily on the Doctor's past, specifically the trappings of the early-70s 'UNIT era' in the form of Bessie, Brigadier Lethbridge-Stewart and UNIT itself. Indeed, specific elements of *Battlefield* recall individual stories from 1971, with UNIT's guardianship of a nuclear missile convoy reprising the scenario of *The Mind of Evil*[45] while the involvement of a witch, a demon and science disguised as magic recalls *The Dæmons*. Born in 1964, Aaronovitch has admitted that 'I'd always wanted to do a UNIT story. It was my era of **Doctor Who**'[46]. Even in his later career as a bestselling novelist, the basic idea of a forces detachment tasked with protecting the realm from otherworldly threats arguably informs the setup of his **Rivers of London** books, whose protagonist, DC Peter Grant, belongs to a division of the Metropolitan Police dealing with magical crime.

Both *Battlefield* and *Remembrance* have an additional agenda of extending the known history of UNIT beyond the context established in those earlier stories. Thus, the near-future iteration of the taskforce Aaronovitch envisages in *Battlefield* is the

---

[45] Technically *The Mind of Evil*'s Thunderbolt missile is a nerve gas warhead mounted on a nuclear-**powered** rocket, rather than a nuclear bomb per se, but it is referred to as a 'nuclear missile' nevertheless (*The Mind of Evil* episodes 2, 3).

[46] Quoted in Cartmel, *Script Doctor*, p153.

counterpart of the precursor organisation he created for *Remembrance*, while the Intrusion Countermeasures Group's Group Captain Gilmore is as clearly Lethbridge-Stewart's 1960s forerunner as Winifred Bambera is his 1990s successor.

Aaronovitch states that he 'wanted to rehabilitate the Brigadier, who had tended to be presented as a bit of a buffoon [...] and I wanted to make UNIT credible'[47]. The future history of UNIT and its personnel is a topic to which he would return in his **New Adventures**, where, as in *Battlefield*, his approach emphasises the underlying geopolitics of the United Nations, its polyethnic makeup, the potential of influential individuals to become an aristocratic elite, and the long view of global history[48]. It is a perspective which expands UNIT's context from the parochial setup seen in the 1970s, where its troops and officers generally seemed to hail from the same English home counties routinely targeted in alien invasions. While such an amplified treatment of UNIT is both characteristic of Aaronovitch and well suited to the Afrofuturist aesthetic of the **New Adventures'** future history, it also exemplifies

---

[47] Quoted in Cartmel, *Script Doctor*, p151.

[48] Aaronovitch's **New Adventures** introduce Kadiatu Lethbridge-Stewart, a recurring character whose ancestors are African UNIT officers descended from the child of the young Alistair's affair with a Sierra Leonean woman (Aaronovitch, Ben, *Transit*, pp7, 124, 181-84). A one-off character, Genevieve ap Gwalchmai, appears to be a distant descendant of Bambera and Ancelyn (Aaronovitch, Ben, and Kate Orman, *So Vile a Sin*, pp29, 165). *So Vile a Sin* suggests that UNIT will eventually become 'the Unitatus', a multi-species pseudo-religious chivalric order somewhat reminiscent of **Babylon 5'**s 'Rangers' (Aaronovitch and Orman, *So Vile a Sin*, pp134, 197-98).

Doctor Who's evolving view of its own past, present and future during Andrew Cartmel's time as its Script Editor.

Let's Kill Thatcher

The influence of Cartmel's script-editorship on the kinds of stories **Doctor Who** told in the late 80s can be seen in a number of related strands, all particularly visible in the other three stories of 1989, which continued both into the **New Adventures** and, to some extent, into 21st-century televised **Doctor Who**.

One of these was an increase in the expected level of thematic depth in each story. While earlier **Doctor Who** had produced exceptional stories which demanded greater intelligent engagement on the audience's part – *Warriors' Gate* (1981) and *Kinda* (1982) spring to mind – it was unprecedented for a run of stories to show such consistent complexity as we see in the majority of stories between *Dragonfire* and *Survival*. The depth of *Battlefield*'s themes will be addressed in the remainder of this book, but it will be useful to look at three other trends of the 'Cartmel era' here.

One of these is that the series' political engagement – often visible previously in the form of rather generalised allegory – can be seen morphing into more pointedly barbed political satire against contemporary attitudes, and particularly against the Conservative government under Margaret Thatcher[49]. Cartmel notoriously

---

[49] Thatcher (1925-2013) was leader of the Conservative party from 1975, and Prime Minster from 1979, until her resignation in 1990. For more on **Doctor Who**'s response to her premiership, see Chapter 1 of McCormack, Una, *The Black Archive #23: The Curse of Fenric*.

stated in his interview for the script editor position that his ideal achievement would be for **Doctor Who** to '[o]verthrow the government'[50]. By 1989, Thatcher had been in power for a decade, and the trend of increasingly overt political commentary had begun some time before Cartmel took over[51]; but it was never as blatant as in *The Happiness Patrol*, where the planetary tyrant toppled by the Doctor was written and played as a thinly-disguised analogue of Thatcher, or *Survival*, where the consequences of the social Darwinist philosophy her government espoused could be observed on a contemporary housing estate as well as on an alien world[52]. Less obviously topical stories like *Remembrance*, *Ghost Light* and *The Curse of Fenric* were savagely critical on such topics as racism, organised religion and war, and even *The Greatest Show in the Galaxy* can be read politically as a story of the hippie generation of the 1960s surrendering their ideals to the capitalism of the Reagan-Thatcher era.

I will show in a later chapter that *Battlefield* engages peripherally, but in occasionally radical ways, with national and global politics. However, it is notably reticent on the question of which party governs its near-future Britain, and on what political platform. Even Lavel's suggestion that she and Lethbridge-Stewart might be expected to pay for the helicopter that Morgaine has destroyed

---

[50] Quoted in McCoy, Sylvester, 'Foreword' to Cartmel, *Script Doctor*, p7.

[51] See Cooray Smith, James, 'Lenny Henry for Doctor Who', for some examples from the 1985 season.

[52] *Ghost Light* can also be convincingly read as a critique specifically of **social** Darwinism: see Dennis, Jonathan, *The Black Archive #6: Ghost Light*.

appears to relate to UN rather than British bureaucracy[53]. If Morgaine is intended as a Thatcher analogue, she is a significantly subtler one than *The Happiness Patrol*'s Helen A, and though like A she ends up broken and in tears, she repents of her villainy in a way A never does.

Battlefield's cast makes a different kind of political statement, in that the story's near-future setting allows it to demonstrate ethnic diversity more effectively than period stories such as *Ghost Light* and *The Curse of Fenric*[54], featuring a black character and an east Asian character, neither of whom is defined by their background, and one of whom apparently enters an interracial relationship. It also portrays racism directly, in a way it would be surprising to see in the series today, when Ace, under grave stress exacerbated by Morgaine's influence, snaps and yells racial epithets at her friend Shou Yuing[55]. That these are out of character for her is obvious, both from her immediate reaction and from her response to racism in other stories (most clearly in *Remembrance* and the backstory to *Ghost Light*), and she concludes that 'Someone's playing games with our minds.'[56] However, the acknowledgement that terrified people may do and say things their calmer selves would abhor might be read as a moment of unusually brutal emotional honesty.

---

[53] *Battlefield* episode 2.

[54] Although 21st-century **Doctor Who** has largely overcome such scruples, and has tended to use ethnically diverse casts in period stories as well.

[55] This is not to say that characters in 21st-century **Doctor Who** are never overtly racist, though they rarely are; it is difficult to conceive that a 21st-century companion might express themself as Ace does, even under equally extreme circumstances.

[56] Episode 3.

Battlefield's most defiant political stance, however, comes in the Doctor's polemic against the use of nuclear weapons. Cartmel called this 'the CND speech', and some 20 years later, when the British press unexpectedly dredged up the politics of late-80s **Doctor Who** as evidence of historical BBC anti-conservative bias, it was widely reported that he had based it on material produced by the Campaign for Nuclear Disarmament, which had had cause to be particularly vociferous during the Thatcher years[57]. Cartmel himself says that the imagery was inspired by the BBC TV play *The War Game*, made in 1965 but considered 'too horrifying for the medium of broadcasting' in the UK until 1985[58]. He also says that, while Aaronovitch 'certainly didn't disagree with the sentiments', the reason Aaronovitch handed the writing of this speech over to him was that he had had enough of 'the rhetoric' from his politically active family[59]. The danger of nuclear destruction is a theme to which Cartmel has returned in his later work[60].

The second trend visible under Cartmel is what he refers to as 'restoring the mystery' of the Doctor – deconstructing what by now was known about his background and character, and substituting suggestions of a deeper, more enigmatic past and a more questionable set of present motivations. In this respect

---

[57] Episode 4; Cartmel, *Script Doctor*, pp158-59; Horne, Mark, 'Doctor Who in War with Planet Maggie'.
[58] Cartmel, *Script Doctor*, pp158; 'BBC Film Censored?'.
[59] Cartmel, Andrew, and Carl Rowlands, '**Doctor Who**: 50 Years of Nasty Things and Groovy Monsters'.
[60] For instance in his BBC **Doctor Who** novel *Atom Bomb Blues* (2005) and his **Doctor Who: The Seventh Doctor** comic story *Operation Volcano* (2018).

Aaronovitch's *Remembrance*, in which the Doctor commits genocide with an ancient weapon he stole before leaving Gallifrey and may have played a part in inventing aeons earlier, is a trailblazer. Other stories of the era, such as *The Greatest Show in the Galaxy* and *The Curse of Fenric*, give the Doctor history with mythical or divine beings which itself approaches the status of legend, while also showing him more consciously manipulating the responses of those around him to serve his plans.

Cartmel felt that by 1987 the Doctor's character had become too familiar and comfortable:

> 'that initial mystery [...] had been eroded over the years as viewers learned that the Doctor was something called a Time Lord, that there are a load of other Time Lords, that he's not even in charge, that he can be put on trial, until he's just a midget version of the fantastic character he was when it started with scary old William Hartnell.'[61]

In point of fact, all of the revelations Cartmel cites occurred over the space of a handful of episodes in the middle of 1969[62]. Cartmel's reference to erosion 'over the years' suggests that he is perhaps thinking instead of the repeated use of Gallifrey as a setting and Time Lords as characters during the 1970s and 80s, culminating in the Doctor's **second** trial in *The Trial of a Time Lord* (1986).

---

[61] Cartmel, *Script Doctor*, p93.
[62] In episodes 6 to 10 of *The War Games* (which should not be confused with *The War Game*).

Nothing we see or learn in *Battlefield* calls the Doctor's past into question – indeed the UNIT material actively canonises it. The story approaches Cartmel's project of remystification obliquely, thanks to its premise of the Doctor's future 'com[ing] back to bite him in the arse'[63]. While not pronounced enough to count as a prevalent trend (and certainly not as pronounced as it would become during 2010-17, Steven Moffat's time as showrunner), it is noticeable that the stories of the Cartmel era are more willing to play narrative tricks with time-travel than earlier **Doctor Who**. In both *Ghost Light* and *The Curse of Fenric*, for instance, Ace will carry unwelcome memories from her childhood into portions of the historical past where they take on the status of foreknowledge. Here the reverse is true, with the Doctor unable to remember events from his life which are history to Morgaine, Mordred and Ancelyn.

Thus, although this is another story where the Doctor interacts with figures of myth, his role in the legends is not part of his backstory but something still to happen to him, and he is initially as bewildered as the other characters by the part his future self expects him to play in current events. He learns fast, however, quickly realising that he can bluff his way through the plot by assuming the role of Merlin and turning the situation to his own advantage; and he reveals disconcerting foreknowledge of his own when he exclaims that Lethbridge-Stewart is 'supposed to die in bed'[64]. The suggestion is that the path of character development he is currently following is one that will naturally lead to him becoming the Machiavellian Merlin of his personal future.

---

[63] Cartmel, *Script Doctor*, p150.
[64] The character's eventual reported death in *The Wedding of River Song* (2011) sounds as if it conforms to this expectation.

A third, related trend is a burgeoning interest in the emotional life of the companion and her relationship with the Doctor, as well as to a lesser extent in the emotions and relationships of the supporting cast. Again, this perhaps involved to some extent recapturing the flavour of the very earliest **Doctor Who** stories. The dynamics of the growing trust, friendship and even implicit romance between the original regulars – Ian, Barbara, Susan and the first Doctor – had been an important element of the series' early years, but such subtleties had largely been abandoned by the late 60s. In general the emotions most often evinced by the companions since then had been action-story responses of horror, fear, excitement, anger, surprise and the like.

While Ace's friendship with the Doctor has none of the potential for romance that has informed many of the Doctor's significant associations since, it is nevertheless both tender and turbulent, not unlike parenting a teenage child. The Doctor's moral authority is called into question by the mistakes and missteps he makes in mentoring her, while Ace herself experiences a gradual blossoming from story to story, rather than undergoing change only in her introductory and final stories like some of her predecessors. *Battlefield* is perhaps not a standout example of this relationship compared with its 1989 peers, but it does show the Doctor quizzing Ace on Clarke's Law and the origins of electromagnetic pulses, trusting her with the dangerous task of safeguarding Excalibur and, finally, factoring her disobedience into his plans as 'an Ace up my sleeve'[65].

---

[65] *Battlefield* episode 4.

Beyond this, *Battlefield* is unusually willing to show tender emotions on the part of its characters, even if its knightly lover and his paramour are less than fully effective. The Rowlinsons and particularly the Lethbridge-Stewarts are convincing as married couples, both in the writing and the performance, and Morgaine is a particular study in emotional contrasts. Her ruthlessness and even cruelty to her enemies stands against her fondness for her son and her sense of loss for the dead Arthur. *Battlefield* may not be unique as a **Doctor Who** story in which the villain turns out to be driven primarily by a warped romantic love, but it is rare in this regard. That the story's villains are mother and son is also unusual in the context of **Doctor Who** as a whole, but unexceptional in the context of Cartmel's three years as script editor, which saw a significant upturn in the depiction of family relationships, including in every story of 1989[66].

'Our Last Battlefield'

A separate but relevant question, when looking at *Battlefield* in the context of the 1989 season of **Doctor Who**, is whether the story was always intended as the sole appearance of Brigadier Bambera's near-future UNIT, or whether these characters might have become a recurring element of TV **Doctor Who** in the 1990s, like their 1970s predecessors under Lethbridge-Stewart, or indeed their 2010s successors under his daughter Kate. As previously noted, UNIT was not present in Aaronovitch's earliest story concept, but

---

[66] Other than Morgaine and Mordred, there are Mrs Pritchard and Gwendolen in *Ghost Light*, Kathleen and Audrey (and Ace) in *The Curse of Fenric*, and Midge and Squeak in *Survival*.

its involvement arose early on, and such an intention might easily have emerged by the script development stage.

A summary of the 1989 season in the recent *Doctor Who: The Complete History* partwork notes that 'the tantalising prospect of [Lethbridge-Stewart's] death and the introduction of a new Brigadier who couldn't be more different from him suggests a series striding boldly forward,'[67] and indeed there is no shortage of reasons to imagine that Bambera might have returned. In addition to her descendant's appearance in *So Vile a Sin*, the character appears, married to Ancelyn, in two **New Adventures**, *Head Games* (1995) by Steve Lyons and *The Dying Days* (1997) by Lance Parkin[68]. She is described as returning in 'What If?', a counterfactual account of the TV series' continuation into the early 1990s based on interviews with Cartmel and other creative personnel and published in *Doctor Who Magazine* (DWM) #255 (cover date August 1997). And Angela Bruce did in fact reprise the part in 2011 in *Animal*, one of a sequence of four audio dramas, again notionally continuing the Doctor's adventures from the end of the 1989 season, which were commissioned and edited, and in *Animal*'s case also written, by Cartmel.

However, while the **New Adventures** were the official continuation of **Doctor Who** in the early 1990s, they are not especially indicative of Cartmel's superseded intentions for the TV series. While Cartmel, Aaronovitch and Marc Platt contributed background material for the books, editorial control of the series was assumed

---

[67] *The Complete History* volume 45, p97.
[68] Lyons, Steve, *Head Games* pp191-94; Parkin, Lance, *The Dying Days* pp49, 127.

by employees of Virgin Publishing. The books these three wrote were subject to the publisher's creative direction and decisions, and as none of them was involved in *Head Games* or *The Dying Days*, neither can stand as proof of their intentions for Bambera had the TV series continued[69].

Stronger evidence might be found in the DWM feature, published in the summer of 1997 after the **New Adventures** had finished (at least in their **Doctor Who** iteration). Over the course of nine pages Dave Owen interviewed John Nathan-Turner, Cartmel, Aaronovitch, Platt and others about plans for post-1989 stories under the title '27 Up', and used their comments to create a speculative account of two further seasons that might have been broadcast in 'What If?'. The hypothetical stories Owen outlines include 'Animal', which involves animal rights activists breaking into an experimental lab, and 'Network', in which Bambera helps the Doctor deal with the Rani (last seen in 1987's *Time and the Rani*) and a 'biological computer virus', on a university campus. However, while elements ascribed to 'Animal' are described in the interview with Cartmel incorporated into '27 Up'[70], none of those detailed in 'Network' – the campus, the computer virus, the appearances of Bambera and the Rani – are mentioned by any of the interviewees.

In fact, while much of 'What If?' is closely based on the interviews (though taking little account of the likely impact on the stories of compromises and collaborative input beyond the scripting stage,

---

[69] Both books include brief acknowledgements sections; none of the trio is mentioned in either.

[70] The animal rights activists and the experimental lab also appear in a different form in Cartmel's **New Adventure** *Warlock*.

like Kerrigan and Nieradzik's influence on the look of *Battlefield*), other aspects are more speculative. Dave Owen confirms that Bambera's appearance in his counterfactual 1992 season was a piece of creative interpolation on his part:

> '[Cartmel] definitely never mentioned bringing back either characters from his watch or immediately beforehand. In my spun-up seasons, I took the approach that reuse of familiar elements would promote believability. I think the setting of "Network" is a direct lift from *Downtime* which would have resonated with readers at the time, for example.'[71]

Some 14 years later Big Finish released the Cartmel-curated quartet of audio dramas which supposedly represented his unmade post-1989 season, as part of its wider **Doctor Who: The Lost Stories** series[72]. These were written by Cartmel, Aaronovitch and Platt, and drew on a number of the story concepts outlined in the DWM article. *Animal* uses the basic outline ascribed in 'What If?' to 'Animal', but incorporates from 'Network' both the campus setting and Bambera's UNIT force (though not the Rani).

Cartmel's 'Production Notes' for *Animal* seem at pains, however, to emphasise that this had not been his original plan:

---

[71] Owen, Dave, private correspondence with author, 11 March 2018. *Downtime* (1995) was a straight-to-video spinoff story written by Marc Platt. As it happens, the 1996 novelisation by Platt includes a cameo appearance by Bambera.

[72] They are *Thin Ice* by Platt (unrelated to Sarah Dollard's 2017 **Doctor Who** TV story of the same name), *Crime of the Century* and *Animal* by Cartmel, and *Earth Aid* by Aaronovitch and Cartmel. Some of the other stories mentioned in 'What If?' and '27 Up' have also been adapted for non-TV media.

'I realised that the period of the story and the presence of UNIT gave rise to a very interesting possibility. And on 26 November 2009 I sent an email to producer David Richardson saying, "There could even be a part for Bambera (Angela Bruce). Am I nuts?"'[73]

Both the surprise Cartmel expresses here and his careful noting of the date seem like fairly firm assertions that he, at least, had not considered Bambera as a potential returning character until some 20 years after *Battlefield* was broadcast.

Inevitably, various factors – including the passage of more than two decades, the change in medium, and the pressures of Big Finish continuity[74] – mean that the **Lost Stories** releases also cannot be considered an accurate reflection of what another season of Cartmel's **Doctor Who** would have been like. Indeed, Dave Owen suggests that one such factor was the influence of his own 'What If?' on the audience's, and thus the producers', expectations:

> 'It all gets a bit circular by 2010-11 when [Big Finish] feed Cartmel my story titles to work from, even though he doesn't like them […] I now feel that in coupling research and spin as I did in 1997, I really made the process of researching the subject more chaotic and unreliable than it was before.'[75]

---

[73] Cartmel, Andrew, 'Production Notes', *Animal* CD inlay card.

[74] Most noticeably, Ace does not leave during *Thin Ice*, which according to 'What If?' / '27 Up' she would have done, but remains with the Doctor in line with multiple Big Finish stories.

[75] Owen, private correspondence with author, 11 March 2018.

Although Cartmel's own words in '27 Up' are presumably reliable, we should thus be wary of placing much more reliance on 'What If?' and the **Lost Stories** as expressions of his intentions for 1990s **Doctor Who** than we do on the **New Adventures**. As far as Bambera's return is concerned, the evidence of *Animal* suggests that Cartmel would not have obstructed it had the possibility arisen organically – in the same way that the recurring character of Glitz was incorporated into the revised outline of *Dragonfire* under his script-editorship, or indeed Lethbridge-Stewart into that of *Battlefield* – but it also seems that there were no firm plans in this direction.

We should therefore consider Bambera, Ancelyn, Zbrigniev, Husak and the other UNIT personnel as *Battlefield*'s guest characters, rather than as semi-regulars denied their chance to recur.

CHAPTER 3: 'THIS THING ABOUT KING ARTHUR'

Doctor Who is as eclectic in its use of 'world mythology' – as distinct from widely-practised living faiths like Christianity and Buddhism – as it is in drawing on its many other sources. It also approaches this mythical material in various ways

One method is to construct a science-fiction story with parallels to a myth – more often than not a classical myth – and usually to flag the fact in dialogue. This is the approach taken to, for instance, the myths of Jason and the Golden Fleece in *Underworld* (1978), the Minotaur in *The Horns of Nimon* (1979-80) and the Minotaur again in *The God Complex* (2011). Another is to suggest that elements of various mythologies are real, but explicable through science fiction tropes, generally ancient visitations by aliens – the view taken of the Titan Kronos (and the Minotaur again) in *The Time Monster* (1972), the Egyptian god Set in *Pyramids of Mars* (1975), and the apocalypse-heralding Norse monster Fenrir in *The Curse of Fenric*. (This is also a common approach to invented alien religions, for instance in *The Face of Evil* (1977) and *Planet of Fire* (1984).) A third variant consists of stories where, rather than inspiring a myth, the alien takes advantage of an existing one to deceive the superstitious locals. In the earliest example of this, *The Myth Makers* (1965), the alien masquerading as Zeus is the Doctor himself; a more recent one is the Mire warlord who impersonates Odin in *The Girl Who Died* (2015).

As this list suggests, such myths as are used are generally those which a British audience with a casual interest in mythology might be expected to find familiar: classical myth is by far the most frequent, with occasional digressions into the Norse and Egyptian mythoi, and smatterings of other world mythologies here and there (as in *The Talons of Weng-Chiang* (1977)). Where Christianity is used as a source, the focus is on the more overtly mythical and less spiritual elements, such as angels (whose treatment in *Ghost Light* belongs to the second approach above) or the Devil (similarly given the 'ancient alien' treatment in *The Dæmons*) – steering well clear of personal appearances by Jesus or the Christian God.

A parallel to this selection of subject-matter can be found in the roster of popular retellings of myths for children written in the 1950s and 60s by Roger Lancelyn Green, from which some viewers (including the current author) would have gained much of their knowledge of mythology – and whose name is echoed, consciously or otherwise, in that of *Battlefield*'s Ancelyn. Lancelyn Green's output for Puffin Books includes two volumes recounting Greco-Roman legend and one each based on Norse and Egyptian myth[76]. Though Lancelyn Green did not write on the Christian mythos, his output roughly mirrors the frequency with which these other bodies of legend crop up in **Doctor Who**.

With this background in mind, it seems surprising that it took televised **Doctor Who** 26 years to produce a King Arthur story. The

---

[76] Respectively *Tales of the Greek Heroes: Retold From the Ancient Authors* (1958), *The Tale of Troy: Retold From the Ancient Authors* (1958), *Tales of the Norsemen: Retold from the Old Norse Poems and Tales* (1960) and *Tales of Ancient Egypt* (1967). A modern parallel is Rick Riordan, whose young adult fantasy books in the **Percy Jackson** series draw primarily (and extensively) on classical mythology, but are supplemented by trilogies featuring the Egyptian and Norse pantheons.

first of Lancelyn Green's books of legends for Puffin was *King Arthur and His Knights of the Round Table* (1953), and these stories are quite as familiar to British audiences as those of the Greek heroes; certainly far more so than the Celtic myths from which they sprang. Indeed, it seems likely that more viewers of **Doctor Who**, abroad as well as in the UK, would have heard stories of Merlin and Morgan le Fay than would be familiar (at least without the programme's influence) with those of Set or Fenrir.

Even so, Arthurian references are rare in TV **Doctor Who**, let alone more substantial manifestations. Direct allusions prior to 1989 are confined to a cameo appearance by an explicitly fictional Sir Lancelot in *The Mind Robber* (1968)[77], and Mike Yates in *The Time Monster* describing an apparition of a medieval knight as 'You know, sir, the King Arthur bit.'[78] Since *Battlefield*, a couple of Arthurian names have appeared in equally casual contexts: the Guinevere 1 space probe, named for Arthur's queen, in *The Christmas Invasion* (2005); and the Fisher King, named after the perennially wounded keeper of the Holy Grail, in *Under the Lake / Before the Flood* (2015). The former name appears to be used simply to mark the probe as British (though Russell T Davies reuses it for a satellite monitoring network in *Turn Left* (2008), possibly implying that the same company has created both technologies). In the second case, the fact that the armoured alien warlord is found inert in a spaceship under a lake suggests – rather unexpectedly – that the Arthurian reference could potentially be a nod to *Battlefield*.

---

[77] *The Mind Robber* episode 5. Episode 3 of this story features yet another Minotaur, this one also fictional.
[78] *The Time Monster* episode 3.

The most detailed prior use of Arthurian myth in TV **Doctor Who**, though so allusive it might well have passed most viewers by, is in *The Stones of Blood* (1978), written by David Fisher, which also represents the series' most substantial use of indigenous British religion[79]. The villain in *The Stones of Blood* is an alien with access to pseudo-magical powers who has spent 4,000 years on Earth, going by various names including several recognisable from Celtic myth[80]. These include 'Lady Morgana Montcalm' and 'Vivien Fay', which together connect her to, and perhaps suggest that she inspired the legends of, both Morgan le Fay and Viviane, one of the names given to the Lady of the Lake[81]. She ends up imprisoned inside (or possibly transformed into) a standing stone in Cornwall, which is remarkably similar to the fate Sir Thomas Malory describes for Merlin at the Lady of the Lake's hands in *Le Morte D'Arthur*[82].

In popular culture beyond televised **Doctor Who**, though, King Arthur had enjoyed a prominent profile during the 1980s. The decade had produced perhaps the definitive film version of the legend and a subversive feminist retelling of it in book form, as well

---

[79] *The Eaters of Light* (2017), the only story to date to deal directly with ancient Britons, crafts its own explanations for their material culture rather than interesting itself in their, or indeed the invading Romans', religious view of the world.

[80] Thier, Katrin, 'Digging Around *The Stones of Blood*', *The Tides of Time* #36, pp10-18. Thier's forthcoming **Black Archive** on *The Stones of Blood* will cover this material in more detail.

[81] *The Stones of Blood* episodes 1 and 2; Lacy, Norris J, ed, *The Arthurian Encyclopedia* p605.

[82] *The Stones of Blood* episode 4; Malory, Thomas, *Le Morte D'Arthur* book IV chapter 1.

as a number of attempts at hybridisation through relocating the themes and characters in the futures of science fiction.

John Boorman's film *Excalibur* (1981) adapted a version of the story distilled from Malory's, with an added vein of pagan mysticism and some elegant elisions which simplified the story greatly. (For example, the sword Arthur pulls from the stone is conflated with the sword given to him by the Lady of the Lake, only the latter of which is traditionally identified as Excalibur.) This presentation centres around its charismatic, capricious and fallible Merlin and his mentor-pupil relationship with its cold and alluring Morgan le Fay (or 'Morgana'); the latter, in betraying her teacher and imprisoning him (here in a crystal prison rather than a standing stone), as well as in bringing up Arthur's illegitimate son Mordred as the king's nemesis, is a powerful driver of the plot. As 'the land and the king are one', Arthur's body itself becomes a battleground, turning Britain into a wasteland after he is wounded.

Marion Zimmer Bradley's *The Mists of Avalon* (1983) retells the Arthurian myth (again largely derived from Malory) from the perspectives of its significant women, primarily Morgan ('Morgaine'), Guinevere ('Gwenhwyfar'), Viviane, Arthur's other half-sister Morgause and their mother Igraine. Bradley's Morgaine is motivated by her allegiance to the old pagan religion and the matriarchal Celtic social order which the patriarchal Roman Christianity Arthur espouses is supplanting. She is the nearest the 1,000-page novel has to a protagonist, and Bradley's attempt to rehabilitate her as a broadly sympathetic figure has been greatly influential on later Arthurian storytellers.

Equally revolutionary, though less widely known, was a 12-issue DC comic series by Mike W Barr and Brian Bolland, *Camelot 3000* (1982-85). Earlier works, notably Mark Twain's *A Connecticut Yankee in King Arthur's Court* (1889) and its multiple adaptations, had taken modern time-travellers into Arthurian Britain, and many books had envisaged the king's return in a present or near future imagined either satirically or allegorically, but Barr and Bolland were almost the first to reawaken Arthur and Merlin in a full-blown SF future. Their quest in the year 3000 is to muster the reincarnations of various Knights of the Round Table, born into ethnically and otherwise diverse bodies, to protect Britain and the world from an alien invasion led by the original, immortal Morgan le Fay and the reincarnated Mordred (Modred). The reborn Lancelot and Guinevere, and Isolde and Tristan (the latter now having the body of a woman) are irresistibly attracted to one another despite their various reservations[83].

Intriguingly, Barr and Bolland's comic was not quite the first to place Arthur and Merlin in a futuristic setting, though the precedent of 'The Neutron Knights' (published in *Doctor Who Monthly* #60 in January 1982) had little impact outside the subculture of **Doctor Who** fandom. Steve Parkhouse and Dave Gibbons' eight-page strip shows the king and wizard in the Earth's far future, defending a fission reactor, 'the Dragon', against the

---

[83] Tristan and Isolde's legend is peripheral to the main body of Arthurian myth, but has been the subject of independent adaptations including an opera by Richard Wagner and a film by Kevin Reynolds. Their illicit love affair, as the knightly champion and royal wife respectively of King Mark of Cornwall, recalls that of Lancelot and Guinevere and may be a source for it.

titular invaders. The fourth Doctor is summoned by Merlin to evacuate them and the other defenders before the reactor explodes and kills the attackers. Other than the identities of these two characters, who have been 'summoned [...] from another time' to 'Earth's hour of need', the story's affinities with Arthurian myth are confined to the aesthetic, with futuristic soldiers kitted out like medieval knights and the reactor building resembling a fortress[84]. ('The Dragon' is presumably also intended as a reference to medieval chivalric legend, although in fact dragons in strictly Arthurian myth are very rare.) Parkhouse and Gibbons' Merlin would reappear in the following comic story, *The Tides of Time* (1982), as one of a council of superior beings named the 'Higher Evolutionaries', but there was no anticipation of Aaronovitch's suggestion that he was the same person as the Doctor.

Equally tangential in its debt to the Arthurian mythos is **Knights of God** (1987), a bleakly dystopian 13-episode ITV children's series written by Richard Cooper, six episodes of which were directed by Michael Kerrigan. **Knights of God** wears its Arthurian influences on its sleeve, naming its elderly rebel leader 'Arthur' and the Prior of the neofascist Knights of God (who turns out to be his son) 'Mordrin'. It borrows from Arthurian myth (perhaps via *Excalibur*) the motifs of a land laid to waste by the absence of the rightful king, and of an island where said king may be sought. However, the king who eventually restores order to the land is neither the character named Arthur nor a resurrected Dark Ages king, but the younger protagonist Gervase, who proves to be the last survivor of

---

[84] Parkhouse, Steve, and Dave Gibbons, 'The Neutron Knights', DWM #60.

the UK's royal family from before the civil war which brought the Knights to power. In fact, despite his family relationship with the villain, Arthur in **Knights of God** is more of a mentor to the character who will become king, and thus a figure more analogous to Merlin.

Although a number of actors (including Christopher Bowen) are shared between the two series, two facts in particular link **The Knights of God** to **Doctor Who**: its other director, Andrew Morgan, had already worked with Cartmel and Aaronovitch on *Remembrance of the Daleks* (a connection explicitly noted, though without comment, in Cartmel's book *Script Doctor*[85]); and the Arthur character who is more of a Merlin character is played by the second TV Doctor, Patrick Troughton. Between these facts and Kerrigan's involvement in both productions, the affinity between the two seems unlikely to be a coincidence.

Overall, these 1980s manipulations of Arthurian myth have little in common beyond their source material, but we may identify some recurring aspects: a playful willingness to rewrite old stories without any great reverence for tradition; a subversive politics manifesting itself in diverse casts and a general scepticism regarding authority; an interest in family and in mentor-student relationships; and a focus on minor or overlooked characters, especially women. All of these are also characteristics of Cartmel's period of **Doctor Who**, suggesting that perhaps the time was ripe for these two strands of popular culture to come together.

---

[85] Cartmel, *Script Doctor*, p151.

The reason it took until 1989 for this to happen may be that **Doctor Who** mythology stories like *The Time Monster, Pyramids of Mars* and *The Curse of Fenric* generally balance the familiar with the foreign: to the audience the myth-systems they depict may be well known, but are not mundane, representing as they do an entirely different set of beliefs from those of either Christian or secular Britain. Just as mythologies that feel too 'exotic' can thin out into a veneer of orientalism (as in *The Talons of Weng-Chiang*), so those which are overly familiar may be deemed insufficiently interesting[86].

Though their Celtic originals date back to the sixth century at the latest, the stories of King Arthur as modern audiences mostly know them went through a thorough process of assimilation to a medieval chivalric Christian worldview in the romances of, among others, Chrétien de Troyes (active between 1160 and 1190), the *Gawain* poet (active in the late 14th century) and Thomas Malory (c1416-71). Although any historical figures on whom the legends might have been based would have died centuries before such things became commonplace, cosmetically the battlemented castles, formal combats and armoured knights of these retellings belong to late medieval England (as Mike Yates' comment in *The Time Monster* suggests), and thus lack the distant fascination of the animal-headed gods of the Nile kingdoms or the monstrous progeny of Loki. The reason there was no 'Doctor Who meets King Arthur' story until 1989 may have been that it would have ended

---

[86] It may be significant that the most direct appearance of a classical deity in **Doctor Who** is that of Kronos, a Titan, rather than one of the perhaps overfamiliar Olympian gods.

up looking much like *The Time Warrior* (1973-74) with no stranded alien, or *The King's Demons* (1983) with no shapeshifting robot[87].

Aaronovitch's earliest ideas for his Arthurian **Doctor Who** story involved 'placing legends in a modern context', circumventing this objection[88]. A reimagined Arthurian mythology, incorporating advanced technology, where battle was joined using guns and grenades as well as swords – and whose look was thus quite different from that of familiar media representations like *Excalibur* or, Heaven forbid, *Monty Python and the Holy Grail* (1975) – was exactly what an Arthurian **Doctor Who** story needed. It was approximately what 'The Neutron Knights' had offered: essentially, King Arthur without 'the King Arthur bit'.

Battlefield is a **Doctor Who** mythology story of the second type: one where the myth turns out to be substantially factual, and explained by science fiction tropes. Though the intruders into our world are not extraterrestrials, they come instead from 'another dimension, sideways in time [...] where the man [Arthur] was closer to the myth'[89] – a distinction which sits well with the legend's Celtic origins, as I will discuss. The story is unclear (even in the deleted 'Clarke's Law' scene) on the question of whether this other world is one where technology merely resembles magic, or one where magic actually works (this, too being a familiar SF trope, though a

---

[87] Matthew Kilburn makes a case for *The Time Warrior* drawing on specifically Arthurian as well as generically medieval sources, but this is not overt in the story as broadcast (Kilburn, Matthew, *The Black Archive #24: The Time Warrior*, pp93-98).

[88] Pixley, 'The DWM Archive: *Battlefield*' p27.

[89] *Battlefield* episode 2.

genre-blending one[90]). Yet even this is largely in line with the treatment of Azal (in *The Dæmons*) and Sutekh (in *Pyramids of Mars*), whose powers are straightforwardly miraculous, however often the Doctor might mention 'psionics' or 'mental force'.

---

[90] See 'Magic', *The Encyclopedia of Science Fiction*.

CHAPTER 4: 'THE LEGENDARY ARTHUR, YES'

By specifying that the other world's Arthur was merely 'closer' to the myth, Aaronovitch absolves himself of any duty to be strictly faithful to his sources. This is useful, as the Arthurian corpus is vast and full of mutually incompatible variations on the same stories. It could never possibly be reconciled into a single continuity, even of the retrospective kind that fan scholars enjoy attempting to construct for **Doctor Who**.

In this chapter I look at the stated and, in some cases, unstated Arthurian affinities of the characters and various other elements in *Battlefield*, summarise the consensus narrative surrounding them in Arthurian tradition, and examine how the story draws on this. Although most of the Arthurian information in this section is widely attested in multiple sources, I have used as my main references *The Arthurian Encyclopedia* by Norris J Lacy (1986) (hereafter 'Lacy'), and Thomas Malory's *Le Morte D'Arthur* (1469-70, published 1485) (hereafter 'Malory'), as these were Aaronovitch's chief sources for the legends[91]. I have supplemented them as necessary with reference to other works.

Place-Names

We never learn precisely where Carbury is[92]. It is definitely in England, and the Carbury Trust is apparently based in Sedgwick[93].

---

[91] Pixley, 'The DWM Archive: *Battlefield*' p28.
[92] A search of Google Maps does turn up two Carburys, but they are in County Kildare and North Dakota respectively.
[93] Episodes 2, 1.

Though it seems a night passes between Lavel and Lethbridge-Stewart leaving Docklands and arriving in Carbury, it is nevertheless within a helicopter journey of London[94]. Bambera thinks it implausible that jets would be flying 'this far south'[95]. Somewhat unusually for a 20th-century **Doctor Who** story with a rural setting, the locals we meet are all too middle-class to have regional accents (though the rehearsal script specifies that Warmsly's is 'Northern'[96]). John Nathan-Turner believed that the story took place in the Lake District, and as there is a Sedgwick in Cumbria this may be the intention despite the visible lack of mountains[97].

What is clear from the story is that Carbury – specifically Warmsly's archaeological dig by the side of Lake Vortigern – is the literal site of Arthur's last battle, which in the legends is known as Camlann. (The name is used only once in the story – spelled 'Camlaan' in the rehearsal script – when Mordred accuses Ancelyn of fleeing the fight that day[98].) It also becomes the scene of the culminating struggle between Morgaine's men and UNIT, a battle which thanks to the nuclear missile threatens to become much more definitively final.

Aaronovitch based the name 'Carbury' on 'Cadbury', a recurring place-name in Devon and Somerset, and in particular on the Iron

---

[94] Episode 2.

[95] Episode 1.

[96] BBC WAC T65/271/1, rehearsal script. James Ellis' performance does not follow this suggestion.

[97] Pixley, 'The DWM Archive: *Battlefield*' p30. As a further data point, Rutland Water where filming took place is in the East Midlands.

[98] BBC WAC T65/271/1, rehearsal script; Episode 4.

Age earthworks named 'Cadbury Castle' at South Cadbury in Somerset[99]. Cadbury Castle's primary claim to fame is that it has for centuries been considered a candidate for the site of Camelot[100]. Rather as an afterthought, the nearby River Cam is sometimes also suggested as a location for Camlann[101]. Camelot goes unmentioned in the broadcast version of *Battlefield*, though the name was used for the military exercise in Aaronovitch's story treatments[102]. While one might conceive of reasons why a canny King Arthur might fight his battles in a dimension separate from his realm (battles being disruptive, unhygienic and often unpopular things), the suggestion that he might site his capital there would make a nonsense of the idea that there was no legendary Arthur in 'our' world, so this aspect of Cadbury's claim is quietly dropped. There is no particular evidence of Iron Age earthworks onscreen, Warmsly's lakeside dig being notably flat.

While the Doctor observes that 'Vortigern' in the lake's name means 'high king'[103], Arthur's traditional title, he fails to mention

---

[99] Pixley, 'The DWM Archive: *Battlefield*' p28. To be clear, there is no castle at Cadbury: castles as we now envisage them were only introduced to Britain after the Norman conquest of 1066. 'Cadbury Castle' is a large artificial earthen mound which would, around the first century BCE, have housed a fortified settlement built in wood.

[100] Lacy pp72-74.

[101] Lacy p73. Lacy spends two pages discussing Cadbury's claim to be Camelot, of which two lines mention the Camlann connection. This is not the same River Cam which runs through Cambridge and appears in *Shada* (1980, unbroadcast).

[102] BBC WAC T65/271/1, 12 and 20 September 1988.

[103] Robert Veermat suggests that the literal meaning is 'overlord'. Though he takes issue with this being equated with 'high king', it

that in the legends it is also a personal name – that of one of Arthur's predecessors, and not one of the more illustrious[104]. Vortigern is known as the king who first allowed the warlike Saxons to settle in Britain, initially to defend the Britons from the Picts and Scots, but who then ceded so much land to their colonies that they became a permanent, and troublesome, fixture. In a **Doctor Who** story with a multi-ethnic cast, which explicitly includes an international peacekeeping force on British soil, this could be significant: indeed, the fact that the story sees both these things in a positive light might have been used to provoke some reassessment of Vortigern's reputation as a bad king. More likely, however, his name is used in the story because of his association with the childhood of Merlin.

In this legend, Vortigern tries to build a tower, but on every attempt it falls down. His magicians advise him that he must locate a boy born without a father and sacrifice him, mixing his blood with the mortar. The boy Vortigern's men find is the young Merlin, who advises him that all his magicians are wrong: in fact the tower is built over a subterranean lake in which two serpents periodically fight, shaking the tower's foundations. The serpents are usually interpreted as symbolising the coming succession of wars between the Britons and the Saxons[105]. It may be significant that beneath

---

seems a close enough idiomatic equivalent for **Doctor Who**'s less academic purposes (Vermaat, Robert, 'The Name of Vortigern').

[104] Lacy pp606-08. Lacy notes that Vortigern seems to have been a historical figure, attested by both the Venerable Bede and *The Anglo-Saxon Chronicle*.

[105] Lacy pp606-07. Some sources (e.g. Geoffrey of Monmouth, *The History of the Kings of Britain* (c1136, trans Lewis Thorpe, 1966)

Vortigern's Lake in *Battlefield* there is indeed a serpent – the spacecraft's automated defence system – and that it is 'Merlin' who discovers it[106].

The lake is also, of course, the resting-place of the late King, which in Arthurian tradition is known as Avalon[107]. Mordred uses the form 'Avallion' when summoning his mother, in terms which could refer to anything from the ruined castle he is standing in to the entire universe where it is sited[108]. The working title 'Storm over Avallion' suggests something towards the more local end of this spectrum.

Two other place-names of Arthurian derivation are used in passing in the story, both like Camlann the sites of battles. One is Badon, where, according to Ancelyn, Merlin 'cast down [Morgaine] with his mighty arts'; Badon, sometimes 'Mount Badon', was the site of a decisive victory by Arthur against the Saxons[109]. The other name is 'Celidon', the wood where Morgaine recalls spending an (evidently romantic) interlude with Arthur[110]. 'Celidon' is the name used in Nennius's ninth-century *Historia Brittonum* for the forest in which Arthur fought his seventh battle against the Saxons; it is also

---

p169) describe the creatures as dragons, rather than the serpents Lacy mentions.

[106] In both versions of the treatment there is more than one guardian, described by Aaronovitch as 'ethereal snakes' and 'Ghost Snakes' (BBC WAC T65/271/1, 12 September 1988 and 20 September 1988).

[107] Lacy pp32-36.

[108] 'To Avallion I summon thee, from beyond the confines of this universe' (episode 2).

[109] Episode 2; Lacy pp37-39.

[110] Episode 4.

used in passing by Alfred Tennyson in his epic Arthurian poem-cycle *Idylls of the King* (1859-85)[111]. It is generally identified with the 'Caledonian Forest' which formerly covered much of central Scotland[112]. It is unclear from Morgaine's reverie whether her tryst with Arthur took place at the time of the battle, or at some other juncture.

The other significant named location in the story (the church's dedication going frustratingly unrevealed) is the Gore Crow Hotel. A 'gore crow' is a carrion crow (the term is used in TH White's influential and imaginative Arthurian fantasy, *The Once and Future King* (1958)[113]), and this ill-omened name is, unsurprisingly, not a common one for British pubs. The naming of the inn is presumably supposed to suggest an oral tradition arising from the ancient battle[114]. However, it also recalls Morgaine's mythological counterpart Morgan le Fay in two different but equally suggestive ways. Firstly, Morgan (according to Malory) married King Uriens, the ruler of a British kingdom of uncertain location, named Gore[115];

---

[111] Nennius, *Historia Brittonum* chapter 50; Tennyson, Alfred, 'Lancelot and Elaine'.

[112] Lacy takes this identification as read without mentioning the 'Celidon' form (p405), and the place-name goes unmentioned in Malory. However, this passage was written not by Aaronovitch but by Cartmel, whose knowledge of Arthurian texts may well have been different (and perhaps recently influenced by James Ellis's adoption of Tennyson quotes for his character).

[113] White, TH, *The Once and Future King*, pp13, 53.

[114] The treatments call it the 'Kings Rest Inn' (sic). In the rehearsal script it is 'The Crowfeast Arms'.

[115] Malory book I chapter 2. Platt's novelisation refers to this Gore (Platt, *Battlefield* p26).

and secondly, the carrion crow is a form taken by the Morrigan, the Celtic war-goddess whose name may well have been the origin of Morgan's own[116]. In the broadcast story Morgaine's romantic attachments, and her predilection for war, are vital character and plot points. It is thus possible that the pub where Morgaine 'gets the tab' is in fact named after her.

The Otherworld

In the science-fiction terms that **Doctor Who** conventionally deals in, Ancelyn's home is 'an alternative dimension', 'sideways in time, across the boundaries that divide one universe from another'[117]. 'Other universes' are rare in televised **Doctor Who**, and coexisting analogues of Earth to which one can travel (as distinct from alien universes physically outside our own, or temporary aberrations of history caused by damage to the timelines which must be corrected) are even rarer. The two clearest examples come nearly two decades earlier, in *Inferno* (1970), and a similar amount of time later, in *Rise of the Cybermen / The Age of Steel* (2006). Both of these feature worlds similar enough that versions of some of the same individuals appear in both, and seem to be based on the idea of 'alternative histories' – albeit ones whose point of divergence is never pinned down. By contrast, for all the rehearsal script implies that there was a historical as well as a legendary Arthur, the possibility that the Merlin of Arthur's world might be the Doctor's

---

[116] Sykes, Egerton, ed, *Who's Who in Non-Classical Mythology* p132; Lacy p395. 'Morrigu', a variant of 'Morrigan', is also among the eclectic collection of Celtic names ascribed to Vivien Fay in *The Stones of Blood* episodes 1 to 2, and she too is associated with crows.

[117] *Battlefield* episodes 3, 1.

alternative, rather than future, self is one which never seems to occur to the Doctor or anyone else. Coupled with the fact that Morgaine can do magic, suggesting different physical laws, this perhaps implies that her world is a true parallel, one echoing aspects of the mainstream universe but which never 'diverged' from it as such, having instead always had its own independent existence.

This concept has certain resonances with some of the oldest Arthurian texts, which display a degree of overlap with pre-Christian Celtic myth. In certain of these, an otherworld sometimes named Annwfn – variously figured as a land of the fay, or of the dead, or of eternal youth, and with some parallels both with the classical underworld and with the Christian heaven – plays a prominent part. Like Ancelyn's home, it is both a realm of magic and a literal country which can be reached by physical, if not necessarily conventional, travel[118].

In Arthurian romances of the chivalric era this conception survives as Avalon, the mysterious place of healing to which the mortally wounded Arthur is taken after his final battle[119]. As discussed, in *Battlefield* 'Avallion' is not the name of the other world, but seems to be the name the inhabitants of that world give Carbury – a location within the primary **Doctor Who** universe. Since Arthur's compatriots must travel across an 'abyss' to reach Carbury, and since Arthur was indeed taken there after his final battle, the suggestion is that from their point of view, it is this universe that is the mysterious otherworldly realm, inverting the standard trope –

---

[118] Lacy pp91-92.
[119] Lacy pp32-33.

although Morgaine seems little awed by its technological wonders[120].

Excalibur

The separate legends of the young Arthur retrieving a sword from a stone, and of him receiving the gift of Excalibur from the Lady of the Lake, are among the best known of Arthurian myths[121]. Taken together they clearly suggest that Excalibur is not, as commonly imagined, the sword in the stone, though texts such as Boorman's *Excalibur* unify the two weapons nonetheless[122].

In *Battlefield* the two are treated as one, at least for the purposes of imagery: the sword that is repeatedly called 'Excalibur' by various parties is kept under a lake, embedded in a control panel resembling a stone block, and Ace pulls it out (though there is no suggestion that only she could have done this) before rising from the lake brandishing it in the traditional manner. There is nothing to tell us that this sword was originally found in either a stone or a lake, however; nor, although Mordred calls it 'brother to Excalibur', is there anything to suggest that his sword is the other one of the pair[123].

Battlefield's most explicit allusions to Arthurian literature relate specifically to Arthur's sword. They come in the form of four quotations from literary sources: one, very brief, from Malory, and

---

[120] Episode 2.

[121] See for instance Malory, book I chapters 5, 25.

[122] Lacy p176. Boorman squares the circle cleverly, by having Arthur throw the sword into the lake after he has broken it through misuse, before the Lady returns it to him restored.

[123] Episode 2.

three of more than a line each from 'The Passing of Arthur', the concluding section of Tennyson's *Idylls of the King*. All four are spoken by Peter Warmsly, and all but the first were incorporated into the broadcast story by the actor James Ellis, on the basis that his character would be familiar with Tennyson's poetry[124].

In episode 1, Warmsly loosely quotes Malory: '**For the scabbard's worth ten of the sword**, said Merlin,'[125] with the Doctor joining him on 'ten of the sword'. Malory's original wording, including Merlin's explanation, runs:

> 'Ye are more unwise, said Merlin, **for the scabbard is worth ten of the swords**, for whiles ye have the scabbard upon you, ye shall never lose no blood, be ye never so sore wounded; therefore keep well the scabbard always with you.'[126]

Malory's Arthur does not keep well the scabbard always with him: it is stolen and later discarded by Morgan Le Fay. If he had followed Merlin's advice, Arthur would presumably have proved much harder to mortally wound at the Battle of Camlann. What, then, the scabbard Warmsly has found is doing at the site of that final battle is a question that is never addressed. (It clearly belongs to Excalibur, as its precipitate attempt to reunite itself with the sword in episode 2 shows.) One can only assume that, in the otherworldly history underlying the legends, either Arthur or Morgaine kept the

---

[124] Pixley, 'The DWM Archive: *Battlefield*' p28; Cartmel, *Script Doctor*, p152.
[125] All emphasis in these quotes is mine, and shows the overlap between broadcast wording and source texts.
[126] Malory, book I Chapter 25.

74

scabbard and conveyed it to the Battle of Camlann, where it was lost. (The legendary Morgan Le Fay has a record of similar behaviour: much earlier in the Arthurian legends she sends her lover, Accolon, into single combat against Arthur armed with the stolen Excalibur and its scabbard, having palmed Arthur off with replicas[127].)

In episode 2 Warmsly moves on to quoting Tennyson to Bambera:

WARMSLY

Did you know that it takes one year to uncover one centimetre on a site this big? **But now delay not: take the sword, and fling him far into the middle mere: watch what thou seest, and lightly bring me word.**[128]

The opening of the quotation creates an ironic juxtaposition, reflecting the fact that Ace has ruined much of Warmsly's painstaking work in her haste to open the tunnel. It also acknowledges that Warmsly is playing for time, having been ordered by the Doctor to guard its entrance.

Episode 3 has two quotations from 'The Passing of Arthur':

ANCELYN

What do you know of Excalibur?

---

[127] Malory, *Le Morte D'Arthur*, Book IV chapter 8.
[128] Warmsly says 'the sword' instead of Tennyson's 'Excalibur'. Since the sword has already been named twice, once in the current episode, there is no reason to withhold its name here, meaning that this is either the character's slip or the actor's.

WARMSLY

King Arthur's sword, Excalibur, wrought by the lonely maiden of the lake[129], who rose up out of the water holding the sword Excalibur aloft.

ANCELYN

This lake?

WARMSLY

Thou rememberest how, in those old days, one summer noon, an arm rose up from out the bosom of the lake, clothed in white samite, mystic, wonderful, holding the sword.

(In the Special Edition he continues the quote – '...**and how I rowed across and took it, and have worn it like a king**' – before concluding with what sounds suspiciously like a reference to **Monty Python**: 'It's all a myth, really. Honestly, women in water holding swords?'[130]) This quote immediately presages the actual emergence of Ace from Vortigern's Lake, carrying Excalibur.

The first and last of these three quotes come from the passage where Arthur asks Sir Bedivere to throw Excalibur into the lake so that the Lady of the Lake can retrieve it. They are out of order but fall close together, separated by two lines:

---

[129] This replaces the words 'Arthur's magical sword, presented to him by the Lady of the Lake' in the rehearsal script.
[130] 'Listen, strange women lying in ponds distributing swords is no basis for a system of government' (*Monty Python and the Holy Grail*).

76

'Thou therefore take my brand Excalibur,
Which was my pride: for **thou rememberest how**
In those old days, one summer noon, an arm
Rose up from out the bosom of the lake,
Clothed in white samite, mystic, wonderful,
Holding the sword – and how I rowed across
And took it, and have worn it, like a king;
And, wheresoever I am sung or told
In aftertime, this also shall be known:
But now delay not: take Excalibur,
And fling him far into the middle mere:
Watch what thou seest, and lightly bring me word.'

The reference to Excalibur's origins comes some 60 lines later, as part of Sir Bedivere's internal monologue during his second abortive attempt to cast the sword into the lake:

'The King is sick, and knows not what he does.
What record, or what relic of my lord
Should be to aftertime, but empty breath
And rumours of a doubt? But were this kept,
Stored in some treasure-house of mighty kings,
Some one might show it at a joust of arms,
Saying, "**King Arthur's sword, Excalibur,**
Wrought by the lonely maiden of the Lake.
Nine years she wrought it, sitting in the deeps
Upon the hidden bases of the hills."'[131]

---

[131] Tennyson, Alfred, 'The Passing of Arthur'.

77

Other than the quality of the poetry itself, what do the Tennyson quotes add to *Battlefield*? The two in episode 3 serve as a brief primer on Excalibur's backstory for viewers who may not be familiar with it (although the image of the sword rising from the lake is surely the best-known and most iconic in the whole of Arthurian lore). The relevance of the quote in episode 2 is more oblique: the story of the sword being **thrown** into the lake scarcely applies in a history where it must have been carefully taken down (presumably through the tunnel) and inserted into the control mechanism of a submerged spaceship. In that it accurately relates the final resting-place of Excalibur, though – and in that 'what thou seest' for Bedivere turns out to be the Lady of the Lake reclaiming it for future use, rather than the sword sinking out of sight forever – it could be read as a tradition preserving something of the historical 'truth'.

The Doctor

'If you're going to do an Arthurian story [...] then the Doctor just has to be Merlin.'

[Ben Aaronovitch][132]

As far as *Battlefield* is concerned, Merlin's identification as a future incarnation of the Doctor is not in doubt. The only reason for any reservation on this point is that, as far as we have seen on TV three decades later, she has not yet become Merlin, and the possibility

---

[132] Quoted in Cartmel, *Script Doctor* p150. 'The Neutron Knights' takes a different view, of course, as does the uncredited short story 'The Creation of Camelot' in *The Doctor Who Annual 1984* (1983), in which Merlin is the Master.

has barely been alluded to since[133]. For the purposes of this story, though, it is independently asserted by Ancelyn, Mordred and Morgaine, and accepted without reservation by the Doctor himself[134]. Several vital pieces of plotting make no sense if it is not the case, beginning with the TARDIS receiving Excalibur's signal and ending with the note Merlin leaves the Doctor in the spaceship[135].

So, if the Doctor is Merlin on a literal level, what does this tell us about his archetypal and symbolic role in the story, and what its creators believe about his archetypal and symbolic role in the series at large?

Other than the King himself, Merlin is the best-known and most central figure in the Arthurian corpus. In the traditional account he is responsible, at least in part, for every significant event of Arthur's early life: his conception; his removal from his parents and his fostering; his discovery of his kingship thanks to the sword in the stone; the gift of Excalibur and its scabbard; and the establishment of the Round Table[136]. As I have noted, Merlin later succumbs to enchantment by a sorceress (often Morgan Le Fay, sometimes the Lady of the Lake) which leaves him imprisoned, asleep or dead, but in any case unable to be of further use to Arthur[137].

---

[133] The Doctor's disappointment following two later regenerations – in *The Christmas Invasion* and *The End of Time* episode 2 (2010) – that he is not yet 'ginger' has been read as a reference to the red-haired Merlin depicted in Platt's novelisation (Platt, *Battlefield* pp6-8), but the implication is tenuous if so.

[134] *Battlefield* episode 2.

[135] Episodes 1 and 4.

[136] Lacy pp382-85.

[137] Lacy pp321-22, 384; Malory book IV chapter 1.

Merlin derives from an early Welsh tradition, in which he was a prophet and bard; his story was only joined with Arthur's by Geoffrey of Monmouth in the 12th century. The reason he figures in Vortigern's story as a child born of no father is that his father is said to have been an incubus, a demon who impregnated his mother in her sleep[138]. (One point of similarity between the two characters – a coincidental one presumably, unless the creators of *Doctor Who* (1996) had both *Battlefield* and some of the less well-known legends of Merlin in mind – is that the Doctor would be revealed, in McCoy's final appearance in the role, to be 'half-human on [his] mother's side', his father being presumably a Time Lord rather than a demon[139].)

The Doctor's function as a wizard, the capacity in which Merlin is best known to modern TV audiences, is obvious, and has been since the earliest days of the series. *An Unearthly Child* (1963) itself shows how the TARDIS is as miraculous to Ian and Barbara in the 20th century as the Doctor's ability to 'make fire come from his fingers' (using matches) is to the Palaeolithic humans they encounter in the deep past[140]. In *Marco Polo* (1964) he is repeatedly called a 'magician' by the Mongol chieftain Tegana, and

---

[138] Lacy pp382-83.

[139] A point in support of this otherwise unlikely reading is that the TV movie's Master refers to Arthurian legend in the very sequence where he learns that the Doctor is half-human, telling Chang Lee, 'You pulled the staff from the stone.' (*Doctor Who* (1996)) This would cast Lee as Arthur and thus the Master presumably as Merlin, but since the story draws unusually close parallels between the Doctor and the Master it could still support the identification.

[140] 'An Unearthly Child', 'The Cave of Skulls' (*An Unearthly Child* episodes 1 and 4).

similar accusations have often resurfaced since[141]. The identification would become almost commonplace during Steven Moffat's period as showrunner, even figuring in the title of *The Magician's Apprentice* (2015); and would resurface as the 13th Doctor, accused of the stereotypically feminine crime of witchcraft, was also related by her title to the Elizabethan magician Dr John Dee[142].

Though the Doctor uses science and technology instead of magic, the technology is often so advanced that Clarke's Third Law would equate the two, and it routinely allows the character to accomplish marvels beyond the abilities of ordinary human beings. The seventh Doctor is more secretive about his techniques than his predecessors tended to be, and at times (notably in *The Greatest Show in the Galaxy*) his abilities seem inexplicable even by the Doctor's established standards. He nevertheless takes a childish pleasure in stage magic, as when he produces a piece of chalk from Ace's ear in *Battlefield* episode 3.

Merlin's role as a prophet finds a parallel in the Doctor's knowledge of the future, based on his experience of time travel: indeed, the Doctor cannot merely tell us the future, but show it to us. In *Battlefield*, his knowledge comes from hints left him by his future self, but we can also imagine how all-knowing this future Doctor could appear in Arthur's time by using the information he gains at Carbury. White's *The Once and Future King* introduced the idea that 'Merlyn' lived his life backwards, 'remembering' the future but

---

[141] For instance in *The Smugglers* (1966), *The Dæmons*, *The Time Warrior* and *The King's Demons*.
[142] *The Witchfinders* (2018).

lacking knowledge of the past. Although Aaronovitch has not explicitly acknowledged White as a source (and Lacy makes no mention of this innovation in his entries on White or Merlin)[143], the idea is a remarkably good fit for the Doctor's dual experience of this story, where Morgaine and Mordred's past is literally his future, and the knowledge he has displayed there is gained through his present experiences[144].

Ace

Merlin's role as Arthur's mentor may have its closest parallel in the Doctor's relationship with Ace. The seventh Doctor enjoys a more pedagogical relationship with Ace than any previous Doctor with his companions, particularly during the 1989 season. He treats her as a pupil, setting her tests and assessing her performance, a practice reinforced by her playfully addressing him as 'Professor'[145]. As far as we know he does not go quite so far as to be present at her conception, but he does enable Ace to send her grandmother and infant mother to a family who will look after them, echoing Merlin's fostering of Arthur with Sir Ector's family[146]. When he returns her to the home she grew up in, it seems she has matured to become a natural leader to her former peers[147]. As the Australian SF author Tansy Rayner Roberts puts it, 'I particularly like

---

[143] Lacy pp382-85, 626-27.

[144] There is also a parallel with, and perhaps an influence on, the Doctor's later relationship with River Song: as she states most clearly in *The Impossible Astronaut* (2011), 'My past is his future'.

[145] *Ghost Light.*

[146] *The Curse of Fenric.*

[147] *Survival.*

that Ace stands in for young Arthur [...] being Merlin's apprentice as well as accidentally drawing the sword from the stone.'[148]

The story does not necessarily imply, however, that Ace is the modern-day equivalent of Arthur. (For one thing, she has no Guinevere, unless we can assign Shou Yuing that role.) It is true that events associate her with Excalibur, as she draws it from its stone channel and finally replaces it there, and is tasked by the Doctor with protecting it from Morgaine during the interim. Her initial removal of the sword is even accompanied by the words 'It's not like I'm King of the Britons, is it?'[149] Excalibur is not solely associated with Arthur, however, and in conveying it to the surface of the lake and handing it to Ancelyn with the words, 'Here, you can be King of England,' Ace appears to be identifying herself as what Cartmel calls 'a funky late 1980s version of the Lady of the Lake'[150]. Indeed, when she arises from the water brandishing the sword immediately after Warmsly quotes Tennyson on the subject, the connection could scarcely be more explicit.

The Lady of the Lake is a slippery figure in the legends, with different names and roles in different stories, but like Morgan le Fay she is often a pupil of Merlin's, and is sometimes the one responsible for imprisoning him, by the use of magic he himself has taught her[151]. One thing that emerges from the interviews in the

---

[148] Roberts, Tansy Rayner, '"She Vanquished Me"'.

[149] *Battlefield* episode 2. Traditionally, Arthur is unaware of his destiny when he pulls the sword from the stone.

[150] Episode 3; Cartmel, *Script Doctor*, p152. Roberts notes that 'She also makes a great 20th Century lady of the lake in her bomber jacket and leggings' ('"She Vanquished Me"').

[151] Lacy pp321-22; Malory book IV chapter 1.

DWM '27 Up' piece is that Ace's character arc would have culminated with her enrolling in the Time Lord Academy, essentially entering training to become the Doctor's successor[152]. To the extent that this longer-term (and possibly as-yet-undeveloped) intention might have influenced *Battlefield*, this suggests that Ace is fated to become, not a new Arthur, but a new Merlin. Aaronovitch wisely follows the simplification seen in retellings such as Boorman's *Excalibur* which ascribes the enchantment of Merlin to Morgan le Fay, not to any of the Ladies of the Lake, but given Ace's often confrontational character we might imagine that as a Time Lord she could in the long run have come to rival the Doctor, albeit with different motives from those of the Master or the Rani.

Brigadier Lethbridge-Stewart

A more obvious candidate for Arthur's role in the story is the Brigadier, who certainly qualifies as having been mentored by the Doctor and whose explicit role in the story is that which legend predicts for Arthur: returning from a long retirement to resume his role as the protector of Britain against outlandish threats[153]. Zbrigniev's reminiscences of his time serving under Lethbridge-Stewart, and the Brigadier's own reference to his 'blood and thunder days', emphasise that he, too, has attained a kind of legendary status, at least among the personnel of UNIT. Given this,

---

[152] '[I]n effect she's becoming Gallifreyan... it turns out that the Doctor wants to enrol her at Prydon Academy on Gallifrey – that's what he's always been leading up to.' (Platt, Marc, quoted in Owen, '27 Up'). In the **Lost Stories** version of Platt's *Thin Ice*, Ace is offered this opportunity but turns it down.
[153] Lacy pp449-51.

the theme of succession here and in *Remembrance of the Daleks*, linking Group Captain Gilmore with Brigadiers Lethbridge-Stewart and Bambera, could perhaps be projected backward through history, making them the latest in a line of protectors of Britain from alien menaces, stretching back to the High King himself (although in the context of *Battlefield* the extradimensional Arthur would have been perhaps as much alien as protector).

This reading would make Alistair Arthur's literal, if distant, successor within the story – indeed, as *Battlefield*'s actual Arthur is clearly not going to be returning, it might be said that the legend of his return is instead fulfilled in the Brigadier. This correspondence would be clearer if Lethbridge-Stewart had indeed died in defence of the realm (as *Battlefield* reveals the 'real' Arthur did); instead he returns to his retirement, as the legendary Arthur does at Avalon.

In this instance, it might seem the man is closer to the legend than the legend himself. If Alistair is Arthur, however, he is blessed with a Guinevere who does not betray him. On the contrary, Doris waits for him faithfully while he is away at his war; and when she does leave him, temporarily, in the final scene, it is for the solidarity of female companionship rather than any adulterous embrace.

Morgaine

From the title 'Morgaine of the Fay', which she uses when trying to intimidate Ace and Shou Yuing[154], it is clear that Morgaine is Morgan le Fay, Arthur's half-sister who is figured as his primary antagonist in many retellings of Arthurian myth. Lacy observes that the presentation of Morgan evolves from 'a powerful and generally

---

[154] Episode 3.

benevolent fay [...] untouched by time,' into a promiscuous witch dedicated to destroying Arthur, before being reclaimed by modern fantasy writers as a more nuanced and sympathetic figure[155].

Though using her as Arthur's (and Merlin's) adversary, Aaronovitch inclines towards presenting her as an eternal, more-than-human being: 'Immortal Morgaine, ageless and deathless'[156]. He also follows Boorman, among other modern sources, in making her the mother of Mordred, traditionally Arthur's bastard son – a function more often ascribed to her sister Morgause, the wife of King Lot of Orkney[157]. The incestuous implications of her romantic attachment to Arthur are glossed over by Aaronovitch – presumably in deference to **Doctor Who**'s target audience – by leaving her sibling relationship with the High King unstated.

Morgaine introduces herself to the Brigadier as 'Morgaine the Sunkiller, dominator of the 13 worlds and Battle-Queen of the S'rax'[158] – titles based in Aaronovitch's SF conception of her home universe, which appear to have no direct equivalence in the

---

[155] Lacy p395.

[156] Episode 2. This characterisation is similar to that of Vivien Fay in *The Stones of Blood* – although there is no evidence that Aaronovitch was influenced by the minor Arthurian elements in the earlier story, and there is certainly no attempt to connect the two characters within the fiction.

[157] Lacy p395; Malory book I chapter 19. When the Doctor confidently identifies Mordred's mother as Morgaine rather than Morgause, he is thus either making a very lucky guess or displaying the kind of inside knowledge he is at pains to disclaim. (Indeed, the same is true of his naming her 'Morgaine', rather than any of the other variants applied to her in the source literature.)

[158] Episode 2.

Arthurian mythos. If the S'rax are indeed that universe's equivalent of the hostile invading Saxons of Arthurian myth, the association between them and Morgan le Fay is not a traditional one. The implication, though, is that the S'rax are Morgaine's own people – in context, presumably humanoid alien invaders of Arthur's Earth – and thus perhaps also the 'Fay' to whom Morgan alludes. If so, it seems unlikely that she would be related to Arthur at all. It is perhaps this background which has allowed Morgaine to survive the 'twelve centuries' to the present day – and which may extend the same longevity to her son Mordred, whom Ancelyn calls a 'half-man'[159].

As Lacy notes, recent Arthurian fantasies such as *The Mists of Avalon* had been keen to rehabilitate Morgan as a positive, or at least ambivalent, character, and thereby question, from a feminist point of view, the patriarchy of the High King's court[160]. Though Morgaine (who uses the same variant of the name as Bradley's protagonist) is the Doctor's antagonist in *Battlefield*, she is not portrayed as evil, but motivated by a set of moral principles alien to the audience – an unusually sophisticated basis for conflict in **Doctor Who** (as much so now as in 1989), and ironically so given the black-and-white nature of the good-versus-evil conflict seen in many Arthurian retellings.

---

[159] Episodes 1, 3.
[160] Lacy pp59-60, 395.

Mordred

After the Doctor / Merlin and Morgaine, Mordred is the third of the living characters in *Battlefield* who are explicitly the same people as figures from Arthurian myth.

In the earliest Arthurian texts Mordred is mentioned merely as another leader with whom Arthur comes in conflict: later accounts make him a rebellious Round Table knight, then Arthur's nephew and, eventually, his illegitimate son by his half-sister[161]. Though *Battlefield* does nothing to commit itself on the question of Mordred's paternity, Morgaine's romantic history with the High King means that the possibility is at least left open. Ancelyn's 'half-man' gibe would certainly seem to suggest that, if Mordred's mother is not human, then his father is (which would be the direct reverse of Merlin's parentage). The fact that Mordred describes his sword as 'brother to Excalibur' might suggest a relationship between their bearers but, as noted, Morgaine has a history of appropriating Arthur's swords for her allies to use[162]. Mordred is frequently portrayed as lusting after Queen Guinevere, Arthur's wife, and in some texts forces her to marry him, either after Arthur's death or merely during his protracted absence[163]. *Battlefield* gives Mordred limited contact with Bambera, its Guinevere equivalent, and when the two meet the crime of Mordred's that incurs the wrath of Ancelyn is his apparent killing of Bambera rather than anything more salacious.

---

[161] Lacy p394.
[162] Episode 2.
[163] Lacy p262.

In the standard version of the legend it is Mordred who kills Arthur at Camlann[164]. Despite his evident prowess on the battlefield, it is difficult to ascribe such a momentous deed to Morgaine's wastrel son – though as *Battlefield* is in part undercutting Arthurian myth (most clearly the promise of Arthur's return), this may be deliberate on Aaronovitch's part. Mordred is portrayed as untroubled by his mother's scruples, drunken, spoiled and frequently pathetic in his reliance on her, and it is clear that, whoever wielded the blade (and despite her belief that he survived), the primary agent of Arthur's defeat must have been Morgaine herself.

Ancelyn

Though it is Ancelyn to whom Ace hands Excalibur after she produces it from the lake, nothing else in the story links Ancelyn directly with Arthur, and he shows no inclination to take up the offer of the position of 'King of England' either before or after Arthur is discovered to be dead[165]. Ace's line can probably be dismissed as the joke it appears to be, rather than having any further significance.

In fact, though straightforward as a character, from the point of view of his Arthurian parallels, Ancelyn is the most ambiguous person in *Battlefield*, having affinities with – and being perhaps an amalgamation of – two prominent yet contrasting Knights of the Round Table. Since the knights in Arthurian myth are numerous

---

[164] Lacy p394; Malory book XXI chapter 4 (though in Malory the battle occurs at Barham Down near Dover).
[165] Episode 3.

and their personalities diverse, their representation by a single character in *Battlefield* warrants this kind of synthesis.

Ancelyn claims the title 'Knight-General of the Britons', but he has come alone to Earth with no others under his command[166]. His reference to '[t]he time of restitution' might suggest that he represents some underground remnant of Arthur's regime, a resistance force against Morgaine's dominance, but this is not explicit in the story[167]. Mordred calls him 'Ancelyn the Craven,' mocking him for having 'fled the field at Camlann', which suggests that Ancelyn, like Mordred and Morgaine, is over 1,200 years old[168]. It is not clear whether the normal human lifespan in his own world is several millennia long (Mordred and Ancelyn both appear to be about 30[169]), or whether this means that he, like them, has some exceptional source of longevity. (Since all concerned consider it possible that Arthur has been in suspended animation for 1,200 years, such technology clearly exists, and may perhaps explain where Ancelyn has been since Camlann.) Though we might assume that he is working to expunge the stain of his cowardice from his knightly honour, this is not implied anywhere except in Mordred's taunting. In fact, his character arc in the story is solely focussed on his burgeoning devotion to Bambera.

The name 'Ancelyn' is occasionally found as a given name or surname, but does not appear in Arthurian legend. Although its

---

[166] Episode 2.
[167] Episode 1.
[168] Episode 4.
[169] Marcus Gilbert was born in 1958, and Christopher Bowen in 1959 ('Christopher Bowen', 'Marcus Gilbert', IMDB).

similarity with the first barrel of Roger Lancelyn Green's family name is suggestive[170], the obvious reason for its use here is its similarity to 'Lancelot': indeed, the second version of the story treatment and the rehearsal script both say explicitly, though wrongly, that 'Ancelyn' is a variant of 'Lancelot'[171]. Cartmel's memoir elaborates:

> 'Incidentally, [Bambera]'s name Winifred is a variant of Guinevere, just as Ancelyn is a version of Lancelot. More power to Ben's battered paperback copy of *The Oxford Dictionary of English Christian Names*.'[172]

Cartmel does not specify which edition of the dictionary Aaronovitch was using in 1989, but examination of a battered paperback copy of the 1977 edition reveals that the various legitimate versions of the name Lancelot 'were often confused with **Ancel** [...] and its diminutive **Ancelot** and **Ancelin**.'[173] This is a shaky foundation on which to claim that the names are equivalent, which may be why the suggestion was dropped.

Sir Lancelot du Lac is a surprisingly late addition to the Arthurian mythos, first appearing in the 12th century, though he quickly became, and remains, one of its most popular characters. Tradition

---

[170] Lancelyn Green's work is mentioned, briefly, in Lacy (p310).

[171] BBC WAC file T65/271/1, 20 September 1988, rehearsal script.

[172] Cartmel, *Script Doctor*, p154.

[173] Withycombe, EG, ed, *The Oxford Dictionary of English Christian Names*, p190. Withycombe notes that the names, though both deriving from Old German, come from different etymological roots (pp22, 190). She does not mention any variant ending in '-lyn', which may make the connection with Lancelyn Green somewhat more likely.

has developed him into a tragic hero, a noble and virtuous knight who seeks perfection, but is brought down – and ultimately brings down the Round Table itself – through his adulterous love for Arthur's queen, Guinevere[174]. Ancelyn's punch-drunk boast that he is 'the best knight in the world' echoes an epithet often applied to Lancelot[175], and Cartmel notes the specific reason why his relationship with Bambera might recall Lancelot's with Guinevere. The shame of his fleeing the battlefield is not one Lancelot shares, but clearly both knights have aspects of their character they must strive to transcend.

However, the full name Ancelyn gives is 'Ancelyn ap Gwalchmai', and this suggests a rather different connection[176]. In Welsh 'ap' marks a patronymic, suggesting that Ancelyn's father was called Gwalchmai. 'Gwalchmei' is an early Welsh name for the character later known in English Arthurian literature as Sir Gawain[177]. Gawain is a more ancient character than Lancelot (who has no identified Celtic antecedent), and generally presented as a more passionate, rounded and human one, struggling to fulfil the ideals of chivalry in the face of personal weaknesses including arrogance, a violent temper and susceptibility to the charms of women[178]. He is also the protagonist most frequently associated with the 'Loathly Lady' legend, in which one of Arthur's knights must lift a curse that has made the woman he is obliged to marry ugly, by granting her the

---

[174] Lacy pp323-25.
[175] Episode 3; Lacy p325.
[176] Episode 2.
[177] Lacy p206.
[178] Lacy pp206-08, Malory book III chapter 7.

thing that women most want – which is 'sovereignty', mastery over their own lives[179].

The sequence in which Ancelyn, refusing to talk to 'peasants', ends up fighting Bambera, before eventually declaring cheerfully 'She vanquished me, and I threw myself on her mercy,' illustrates several of these character traits[180]. Indeed, a family background in which Ancelyn's father had learned to give his mother her sovereignty would stand him in good stead for a relationship with the forceful and independent Bambera. (Gawain's brother Gareth also gladly endures humiliation from a female source when he is assigned as bodyguard to a sharp-tongued and snobbish maiden in the quest to rescue her sister, despite being incognito as a kitchen boy[181].) Gawain is a legitimate son of Morgause and King Lot, and thus Arthur's nephew, but *Battlefield* glosses over this complication, which would make Morgaine Ancelyn's great-aunt and Mordred his first cousin once removed[182].

In Malory, Gawain's oldest son is called 'Sir Gingalin', which does sound faintly like 'Ancelyn', though Gingalin is apparently killed by Sir Lancelot after the discovery of the latter's infidelity[183]. Though neither Malory nor Lacy note the fact, other sources make 'Guinglain' Gawain's son by a fairy, Blanchemal[184] – which, if we assume that Morgaine is immortal because of her own 'Fay' connections, could make an alternative explanation for Ancelyn's

---

[179] Lacy pp375, 623-24.
[180] Episode 2.
[181] Malory Book VII.
[182] Malory book I chapter 3.
[183] Malory book IX chapter 17, book 19 chapters 2-4.
[184] Bruce, Christopher, 'Arthurian Name Dictionary'.

longevity. This strays far beyond the sources we know Aaronovitch used, however.

Brigadier Bambera

In both versions of Aaronovitch's story treatment for 'Storm over Avallion', Bambera ends the story engaged to be married to Ancelyn, and leaves with him for his own dimension. In the second version Aaronovitch gives as the reason for this that 'Winifred' comes from the Welsh name 'Gwenfrei', which is related to 'Guenevere'[185]. This appears to be based on a misreading of *The Oxford Dictionary of English Christian Names*, which (at least in the 1977 edition) correctly identifies 'Winifred' and 'Guinevere' as separate names[186]. 'Winifred' does indeed derive from 'Gwenffrewi', but 'Guinevere' comes from the different name 'Gwenhwyfar'. (While they share the element 'Gwen', which means 'white' or 'fair' but also 'blessed' or 'holy', their second elements mean 'phantom' and 'peace' respectively, so it makes little sense to consider them equivalent[187].) However, the dictionary does append an unexplained 'See also WINIFRED' to the end of its 'Guinevere' entry[188], and it is presumably on this basis that Aaronovitch chose 'Winifred' – rather than, for instance, the etymologically justified 'Jennifer' – as his modern derivative of the Arthurian name.

---

[185] BBC WAC T65/271/1, 20 September 1988.
[186] Withycombe, *The Oxford Dictionary of English Christian Names*, pp140-41, 294.
[187] See (the much more recent) Hanks, Patrick, Kate Hardcastle and Flavia Hodges, eds, *Oxford Dictionary of First Names*, pp115, 277, 429.
[188] Withycombe, *The Oxford Dictionary of English Christian Names*, p141.

In the broadcast version of *Battlefield*, Bambera's connection with Arthur's queen is significantly downplayed, hinted at only in the Doctor's observation that 'There are many secrets in names', on learning hers[189]. This aside, her relationship with Ancelyn (which seems distinctly more ardent on his part than on hers) is the only clear way in which she parallels her supposed original. Even the most sympathetic treatments of Guinevere normally portray the queen as a victim, compelled to marry a man she does not love and thereby kept from the man she does, but most sources agree that she and her lover Lancelot share some of the responsibility for the fall of Arthur's kingdom[190]. Like the majority of women in Arthurian myth, she is generally portrayed as passive, conventionally feminine and reliant on men to support and, when necessary, rescue her. Her betrayal lies in choosing the wrong man within a rigid patriarchal structure: it transgresses against her duty of loyalty to her husband and sovereign, but not against traditional gender roles.

Bambera, by contrast, is an independent agent in her own right: an active soldier in command of men, self-reliant and apparently romantically unattached. Though she never answers Ancelyn when he asks her if she is 'betrothed', we are given no hint that she is betraying anyone, even her duty to UNIT, in forming a relationship with him[191]. An interpretation which placed greater emphasis on Ace's pronouncement of Ancelyn as king might conclude that Lancelot and Arthur are united in the person of Ancelyn, and thus

---

[189] Episode 1.
[190] Lacy pp262-63.
[191] Episode 3.

that this new Guinevere can love him without guilt; but such a weight is almost certainly more than the single line will bear.

Arthur

The legend that the High King might return has been a feature of Arthurian literature since the 12th century, apparently predating it in oral folklore[192]. Malory cautiously reports that 'men say that he shall come again [...] I will not say it shall be so.'[193] *Battlefield* raises this hope repeatedly: when Ancelyn states that Excalibur's call heralds 'The time of restitution; the time when Arthur rises to lead the Britons to war'[194]; when Ace repeats the legend that Arthur is 'In eternal sleep until England's greatest need' (adding the science-fictional speculation that the high king may be 'in suspended animation')[195]; when Morgaine observes that 'without [Excalibur], Arthur sleeps forever'; and finally when the Doctor tells Ancelyn, 'replace Excalibur and Arthur will arise'. However, when Ancelyn does so it is revealed that Arthur has in fact been dead for the 1,200 years since the Battle of Camlann. This undercuts the source material in a way that borders on the brutal, especially in Merlin's curt note to his past self to the effect that 'King died in final battle. Everything else propaganda.'[196] The symbolism inherent in then blowing up the spaceship is quite redundant.

As we have seen, there are again sound reasons for this. A'tur's appearances in the two story treatments gave him a role in the

---

[192] Lacy p449.
[193] Malory book XXI chapter 7.
[194] Episode 1.
[195] Episode 2.
[196] Episode 4.

story's final moments that tended to eclipse that of the Doctor. Merlin may have been Arthur's mentor, but Arthur was Merlin's king, and it is not in the Doctor's character to bow to anyone unless compelled to.

Crossovers between fictional universes can be problematic where the relative statuses of the protagonists are concerned. When the **New Adventures** published a **Doctor Who / Sherlock Holmes** crossover, Andy Lane's *All-Consuming Fire* (1994), its effect was to diminish Holmes, whose compendious but context-specific understanding of Victorian England is useless to him in the face of the Doctor's wider universe. (Steven Moffat, showrunner of **Sherlock** for the BBC as well as **Doctor Who**, wisely resisted the temptation to join his two fictional universes[197].) When the Doctor meets Gulliver in *The Mind Robber*, the latter is explicitly a fictional character lacking in agency and autonomy. *Robot of Sherwood* (2014) makes a major point throughout of the heroic rivalry between the Doctor and Robin Hood, but this could hardly have been explored fully in the final minutes of *Battlefield* episode 4.

By writing the living Arthur out of his final draft, Aaronovitch avoids such a conflict. In the broadcast version, Arthur's role is filled by the Brigadier, whose relationship with the Doctor as a complementary and roughly equal authority is well-established by tradition and precedent. Though his props and supporting cast are present throughout *Battlefield*, the eventual decision to keep Arthur himself offstage is for the best.

---

[197] Indeed, *The Snowmen* (2012) frankly disavows the idea that Holmes exists in the Doctor's universe.

The Destroyer

Perhaps in part because of the stories' pre-Christian origins, demons are not a major presence in the Arthurian myths. Malory never uses the term, though he tells of occasional encounters with 'fiends' who appear to be nuisances rather than realistic threats[198]. On two more serious occasions, 'the devil' in the form of an attractive and pliant young woman unsuccessfully tempts two of Arthur's purest knights to become less so[199]. Malory also relays the story of Merlin being 'a devil's son[200]. The Faustian model of sorcerers summoning demons to do their bidding, and of those creatures having the power that the Destroyer exhibits, is almost unknown in the mythos.

Part of the mismatch between the Destroyer and his context is the fact that he stands in the story as a metaphor for nuclear weapons, a supremely destructive force for which the creators of the Arthurian legends were fortunate enough not to need a metaphor[201].

---

[198] See for instance Malory book XIII chapter 12, book XIV chapter 6, book XV chapter 1.

[199] Malory book XIV chapter 10, book XVI chapter 12.

[200] Malory book IV chapters 1, 13.

[201] That said, elements of Arthurian lore are available which might have served. One which springs to mind is the Dolorous Stroke inflicted by Sir Balin on King Pellam, which leaves Pellam permanently injured and for reasons of magical transference lays waste to his realms, killing vast numbers of his subjects in an instant (Lacy p140; Malory book II chapters 25-26). Boorman's *Excalibur* makes the victim of this blow – and its inflictor, bizarrely – Arthur himself, in what may indeed be a nuclear analogy. Such a

In fact *Battlefield* avoids authoritatively naming the kind of being the Destroyer is. Mordred describes him as 'the Lord of Darkness', but Mordred is an inveterate braggart; Morgaine tells Ace and Shou Yuing that he will take them 'to be his handmaidens in Hell', but she, too, is trying her hardest to intimidate; and when Ace calls him Morgaine's 'pet demon', she is evidently influenced by Morgaine's words and the Destroyer's appearance[202]. Unlike *The Dæmons* and *The Impossible Planet / The Satan Pit* (2006), the other **Doctor Who** stories where devils make personal appearances, *Battlefield* leaves no time for metaphysical discussion of the Destroyer's origins, so the possibility is left open that he is merely some kind of alien from Arthur's world who resembles (and perhaps therefore helped to inspire) the Christian conception of demons. The cumulative effect, however, adds up to a strong suggestion that he is exactly what he appears to be.

Intriguingly, Morgaine's reference to 'Hell' is the sole explicit allusion in the story to Christian dogma. A major background assumption in the medieval stories which cemented Arthur's place in world mythology (though not, of course, in their Celtic antecedents), Christianity goes virtually unmentioned in *Battlefield*. Especially, there is no mention or equivalent of the Holy Grail, a central element of Arthurian myth and its most direct link to the

---

relatively obscure reference would not have had the immediate audience recognition factor of a demon, though, nor of those elements of Arthurian lore which *Battlefield* does adopt.

[202] Episodes 3 and 4. Admittedly Mordred also calls him 'Eater of Worlds', which fits with the Destroyer's own statement of his life goals.

biblical narrative[203]. We do not see the detail of the ceremony which Morgaine performs in the churchyard, but it is held at the war memorial, not in the church itself. Notably, it seems to be the names on the memorial which make her realise that it is a sacred site, and not the very visible cross on top of it[204]. The churchyard in *Remembrance of the Daleks* came with its own priest, and *Ghost Light* and *The Curse of Fenric* feature discussions respectively of biblical creationism and of the questioning of faith in time of war, in each case also involving members of the clergy; so this absence is a deliberate choice, not a question of protecting audience sensitivities.

I observed at the beginning of the previous chapter that, for all its assimilation of multiple mythologies, the nearest **Doctor Who** has felt able to come to presenting the explicit trappings of Christianity is the Devil. In creating an almost entirely secular version of a myth where Christianity is traditionally assumed, and making the only visible Christian element a demon, *Battlefield* is a very clear illustration of that trend.

---

[203] Though it has its origins in Celtic myths of cauldrons of healing, the Grail (or 'Sangreal' in Malory) is supposedly a cup used at both Jesus's Last Supper and his Crucifixion (Lacey pp50, 259).
[204] Episode 2.

CHAPTER 5: BUILDER OF WORLDS

Battlefield is set in Britain in the near future, in a carefully unspecified timeframe. The most precise information we get is that it is 'a few years' in Ace's future, but exactly what the Doctor might mean by 'a few years' (or indeed, when he might be counting from, given that Ace appears to have left Earth some time before the series' 'present') is wholly unclear.

Aaronovitch's first treatment for *Battlefield* gives the year as '1999'; the second refers merely to 'the near future', and the vagueness thus introduced continues into the broadcast story. An exchange in the rehearsal script, cut from the broadcast version, strongly suggests that the story's imprecision on this point is deliberate[205]. Platt's novelisation reproduces the conversation:

> She turned back in disgust to the Doctor. 'What year are we in?'
>
> 'Near the end of the twentieth century.'
>
> 'Can't you be more specific? Eighties or nineties?'
>
> The Doctor stared up at the cloudless sky and frowned. 'On the grand scale of things, Ace, what's a decade?'[206]

For what it may be worth, Aaronovitch later told Virgin Publishing, for purposes of **New Adventures** continuity, that the story was set

---

[205] BBC WAC T65/271/1, rehearsal script.

[206] Platt, *Battlefield* p30. Unlike the script, the novelisation has Ace almost immediately spotting that Warmsly's car tax disc expires on 30 June 1999.

in 1997, and the tie-in media have generally followed this timescale[207].

Though such features as pubs, churches and garden centres persist unchanged from *Battlefield*'s 1989 present, certain alienating details serve to emphasise the fictional historical distance between the audience and the setting. In this, *Battlefield* admirably demonstrates the essential science-fiction technique of worldbuilding: not merely imagining a convincing world different from the writer's and readers' own (which many **Doctor Who** stories manage to one degree or another), but the rarer skill of sketching out such a world using a deft modicum of hints and allusions, rather than the indigestible passages of exposition which SF criticism calls 'infodumps'[208].

By comparison, our understanding of Arthur's otherworld is minimal – to the extent that, as discussed, even normal life expectancy is a matter of speculation. We learn that a number of aspects of Arthurian myth are true there, that it probably still adheres to a feudal social system and that its modern inhabitants use bombs, guns and (in one strikingly alien detail) ornithopters[209], but little else beyond what we can infer from a knowledge of Malory.

---

[207] Parkin, Lance, and Lars Pearson, *Ahistory: An Unauthorized History of the Doctor Who Universe*, volume 2 p2156.

[208] See 'Infodump', *The Encyclopedia of Science Fiction*.

[209] Episode 2. An ornithopter is an imaginary vehicle that flies by flapping its wings, widely accepted as being a practical impossibility in Earth's gravity and atmosphere. Whether this suggests that these conditions are different on Morgaine's world, or merely that magic makes such a machine feasible, is impossible to say.

Battlefield's near-future worldbuilding is concentrated in episodes 1 and 2, setting the scene for the coming conflict which naturally takes up most of the later dialogue and action. One of the simplest examples is a simple extrapolation from a recent event: in 1983-84, changes to prices had led to a transition in British currency from pound notes to pound coins, and in *Battlefield*'s future the five-pound note has seemingly gone the same way. Although in reality £5 coins remain outside common circulation as of 2019[210] (and in fact a new design of £5 note was introduced as recently as 2017), the story's prediction of inflation in general is sound enough that modern audiences may need the prompt of Ace's indignant 'How much?' to realise that the price the Doctor's 'five-pound piece' covers – that of a vodka and coke, a lemonade and a glass of water – is grossly expensive by 1989's standards[211].

In taking the near future as its setting, *Battlefield* follows the precedent of its precursors, the UNIT stories of the late 1960s and early 1970s, which share a loose but never quite pinned-down near future milieu in which a British space programme has reached Mars[212], the BBC operates a third television channel[213] and the Prime Minister is likely to be the current leader of an opposition

---

[210] They exist as commemorative collectible items, and are in fact legal tender, but the routine way the Doctor and Pat Rowlinson handle the coin suggests common currency.
[211] Episode 1.
[212] *The Ambassadors of Death* (1970). By the time of *The Android Invasion* (1975) it is aiming for Jupiter.
[213] *The Dæmons*. In reality BBC Three launched in 2003.

party[214], but the designs of such commonplaces as cars, clothing and haircuts remain effectively unchanged from the present. Notably, *Battlefield* takes its cue from the general technique of the UNIT stories, rather than their particular details: episode 1 features a voice-controlled phone, and a matter-of-fact reference to a phone installed in an ordinary civilian car, which are reasonable extrapolations from the telecommunications technology of 1989 but might be seen as a step backwards from the videophones seen in the UNIT stories as early as *The Invasion* (1968) and *The Claws of Axos*[215].

Phones aside, the only other upgraded technology envisaged by Aaronovitch for the use of ordinary Earth civilians in *Battlefield*, a till with integrated computer, appears in the rehearsal script but not the broadcast story[216]. The script has Pat Rawlinson using the device for his accounts, though it has a cash drawer as well as a keyboard and LCD screen. Evidently this is a specialist computer for use in a specific kind of business – the commercial equivalent of an electronic typewriter or dedicated word-processor, perhaps – rather than one that is of versatile and generally applicable function. As with the carphone, what Aaronovitch fails to imagine

---

[214] Based on what can reasonably be assumed to be references to Jeremy Thorpe in *The Green Death* (1973) and Margaret Thatcher in *Terror of the Zygons* (1975).
[215] Carphones existed in 1989 but were luxury items, far from the universals Warmsly's line about 'The one in my car' seems to assume. Automated voice dialling of the kind Aaronovitch envisages would only become widespread in the 2010s.
[216] BBC WAC T65/271/1, rehearsal script.

tells us more about contemporary expectations than what he predicts successfully.

More of the story's innovations are in the sociopolitical rather than the technological arena. Perhaps the most startling of these, especially with 30 years of hindsight, is Lethbridge-Stewart's casual reference in episode 1 to 'the King'. Though there is an irony in the line – the phone call will indeed bring Alistair into the presence of a king, albeit a dead one – the more mundane implication is that Queen Elizabeth II has died (or, given that she was a mere 63 years old when it was broadcast, abdicated) since 1989. Its likelihood notwithstanding, this reference has wider implications, confirming that Britain has retained its monarchy and thus has presumably not experienced a revolution or been incorporated into some larger confederacy, despite its road signs displaying distances in kilometres rather than miles[217].

A king's accession is a one-off event, but on the whole *Battlefield*'s future extrapolates from identifiable trends in its present. The vaguely dystopian military bureaucracy which might hold soldiers liable for the costs of military equipment lost to enemy action, though it apparently belongs to the UN rather than the UK, may still be a comment on the Thatcher government's fondness for introducing the principles of private finance into the public sphere. Less contentiously, the suggestion that the London Docklands might become the site of a heliport evidently arises from the same government's urban regeneration project in effect in the area,

---

[217] Episode 1. British road signs still use miles.

using public and private capital under the auspices of the London Docklands Development Corporation[218].

As a black British woman who is also a senior army officer, Bambera's presence clearly arises from a hopeful extrapolation from longer-term trends towards gender and racial equality which have in reality been rather slower in making inroads into military hierarchy[219]. The direction in her introductory scene plays her identity up as a surprise, showing her approaching, and reflected in, a wing-mirror before she speaks on the radio, so that we first see 'the Brigadier' as a generic military figure in uniform, then see that this officer is black, then finally understand from her voice that she is a woman[220]. Lethbridge-Stewart's later line 'This Brigadier Bambera – good man, is he?' plays the same reversal as a joke, albeit one on Lethbridge-Stewart, whose expectations have failed to move with the times[221].

---

[218] Episode 2.

[219] Army personnel records are personal data and inaccessible to the public, so short of a Freedom of Information request it is not easy to discover when the actual British army appointed its first female brigadier. However, a quick Google suggests that Nicola Moffat, promoted to that rank in 2009, was at the time the most senior female officer in the British army. She is white. (Hopkins, Nick, 'Meet Nicky Moffat, the Highest-Ranked Woman in the British Army', *The Guardian*, 11 January 2012.)

[220] Episode 1.

[221] Episode 2. In the rehearsal script we learn that 'the General Secretary of the United Nations Intelligence Task-Force' (as presumably distinct from the Secretary-General of the United Nations, to whom Doris has spoken on the phone in episode 1) is also a woman, 'Mrs Eva Carlshorst', making Lethbridge-Stewart's

Bambera's presence is only one aspect of the diversity displayed by UNIT troops in the story. She is one of two female officers we see, and though the other soldiers are all apparently white they have surnames and approximate accents which mark them as French (Lavel), Polish (Zbrigniev) and Czech (Husak, whose nationality is stated explicitly)[222]. Zbrigniev (who Aaronovitch in fact intended to be Polish-American) says that he served under Lethbridge-Stewart during the original UNIT era, but the internationalising of *Battlefield*'s UNIT troops is a deliberate 'reimagining of UNIT as a multicultural force'[223]. In 1989, UN high-profile peacekeeping detachments were deployed to countries including Angola, Namibia and Nicaragua, and the Pakistan-India and Iran-Iraq borders, and the personnel of these missions were conspicuously multinational[224]. This may well have prompted Aaronovitch to revise **Doctor Who**'s traditional view of what a UN military taskforce might look like.

Despite their insularity in this respect, the UNIT stories of the 70s did pay attention to geopolitics beyond Britain, with stories such as *The Mind of Evil*, *Day of the Daleks* (1972) and *Robot* (1974-75) addressing projected developments in the Cold War and its associated peace processes. In 1989, *Battlefield* was able to extrapolate from the contemporary progress of reform in the

---

gender stereotyping all the more myopic (BBC WAC T65/271/1, rehearsal script).

[222] Episodes 1 to 3.

[223] Cartmel, *Script Doctor* p153; Episode 1.

[224] Some 66 countries from all inhabited continents contributed troops to these three missions, according to the statistics at 'Past Peacekeeping Operations'.

Eastern bloc, characterised by glasnost and perestroika in the Soviet Union, to imagine a future in which the Cold War is happily over, allowing troops from a presumably post-communist (but evidently still unified) Czechoslovakia to operate under UN auspices in the UK[225]. Taken in conjunction with the adoption of kilometres, this could be taken to imply a greater openness to global, or at least European, sensibility on the part of the British – though Aaronovitch does not go so far as to price the round of drinks in ecus[226]. Certainly the prominence of the UN in the story could be taken to imply a future in which nation states, while enjoying much of their traditional autonomy, are becoming less important while international bodies grow in prominence.

Other events from abroad are reported in dialogue, in a scene cut from the broadcast version of episode 2 but included in the Special Edition. According to Lavel, UNIT's Czechoslovakian detachment has previously been assigned to 'Flood relief in the Low Countries,' while other UNIT troops are 'handling the Azanian ceasefire'[227].

---

[225] Episode 2. Czechoslovakia's 'Velvet Revolution' began in November 1989, between the broadcast of *The Curse of Fenric* episode 4 and *Survival* episode 1. On 1 January 1993 the country ceased to exist, splitting into the present-day Czech Republic and Slovakia.

[226] The 'European currency unit' used for formal purposes, and proposed as the practical single European currency, before the name 'euro' was adopted in 1995.

[227] Both of these functions might be seen as outside UNIT's stated remit of protecting the Earth from extraterrestrial threats – but then so would escorting a nuclear missile convoy, and UNIT had been seen doing that in 1971. The implication seems to be that UNIT troops are routinely assigned to less exotic duties between alien invasions.

Both these details are fruitful in view of the state of the world in 1989.

In 1988 the Intergovernmental Panel on Climate Change had been established, in response to the increasing consensus among scientists that the world was warming as a result of human activity (a phenomenon that had been postulated as long ago as the 19th century)[228]. A few weeks after *Battlefield* aired, Margaret Thatcher (a research chemist prior to her political career) would address the United Nations General Assembly in a speech echoing the warnings of her fellow-scientists about the likely effects on global society[229]. Though Lavel does not give a reason for the flooding in Belgium and the Netherlands[230], evidently assuming that Lethbridge-Stewart will be familiar with it, it does not seem a huge stretch to assume that global warming is involved.

Meanwhile, the anti-apartheid movement within and outside South Africa was gathering momentum, and would lead within a few months of *Battlefield*'s broadcast to the release of the revolutionary leader Nelson Mandela, to the official end of the racist apartheid system within a few years, and eventually to Mandela's election as the country's president in 1994. This is likely the relevance of the reference to an 'Azanian ceasefire', 'Azania' being an ancient Greek term for part of sub-Saharan Africa which

---

[228] Intergovernmental Panel on Climate Change, 'History'; Arrhenius, Professor S, 'On the Influence of Carbonic Acid in the Air upon the Temperature of the Earth'.
[229] Thatcher, Margaret, 'Speech to United Nations General Assembly (Global Environment)'.
[230] 'Holland' according to both story treatments (BBC WAC T65/271/1, 12 and 20 September 1988).

was adopted as an aspirational name for a future free South Africa by various revolutionary anti-apartheid groups[231]. Lavel's passing comment implies both that the name is now internationally recognised and that UN peacekeeping involvement is needed, suggesting a more violent culmination than transpired in reality[232]. Azania is presumably either a post-apartheid South Africa riven by civil war, or an independent breakaway state at odds with the parent Republic. Though this detail was cut from the broadcast story, Andrew Pixley suggests that it informed the performance of Angela Bruce, who decided that 'Bambera was bitter because she had been stuck on the missile convoy as her skin colour had prevented her heading a UN Peace Corps team in South Africa.'[233]

Overall, then, *Battlefield* takes place in a changing world where international conflict and environmental disaster are both significant factors; where, perhaps in response to this, global authorities are growing in influence compared with national ones; and where increasing national, ethnic and gender diversity and

---

[231] Initially by the Pan Africanist Congress of Azania, which formally adopted the name in 1965 having used it in an 'Azanian People's Manifesto' in 1959 ('Azanian People's Organisation (AZAPO)'). The name has historically been politically charged, and one can imagine that its broadcast on BBC One in 1989 would have been contentious.

[232] The rehearsal script has an incomplete news broadcast open with '– positions in the Transvaal', again suggesting armed conflict within South Africa (BBC WAC T65/271/1, rehearsal script).

[233] Pixley, 'The DWM Archive: *Battlefield*' p32. The idea that a white officer would be more acceptable perhaps reinforces the idea that white South Africa still exists and that Azania is a breakaway state, though of course this may be Bruce's interpretation rather than Aaronovitch's.

110

equality are everyday facts of life; but where an affluent western country such as Britain may still retain its currency and system of government, if not its imperial measurements, without apparent contention; where it can carry out ambitious urban redevelopment despite inflation; and where most aspects of everyday life in such a country are affected only by minor, incremental changes in technology and economics.

Yet the script conveys this world though little more than a dozen unobtrusive details of dialogue and design. In many ways *Battlefield* is not a subtle story, but in this respect its subtlety is exemplary.

CHAPTER 6: 'IS THIS WAR?'

Battlefield's title and setting serve notice of a major theme of the story. The archaeological dig on an ancient battlefield tells us what we need to know at the start: in the long run, war creates nothing but a carrion feast for gore crows. The fallout of past conflicts runs through the story, from Badon to Camlann, from the 'blood and thunder days' from which Lethbridge-Stewart has retired to the World Wars commemorated in the churchyard[234].

Given the radical politics of Cartmel's **Doctor Who** and the hawkish record of Thatcher's government (which fought the Falklands War against Argentina, assisted in the American bombing of Libya, housed US nuclear missiles on British soil and commissioned the UK's own Trident nuclear deterrent programme, all over the protests of left-leaning British citizens), it is unsurprising that war, and nuclear war especially, are things of which this story disapproves. This is expressed both rhetorically and in plot terms, from the Doctor's initial revulsion at the nuclear weapon's 'graveyard stench' to his insistence on curtailing the battle between the UNIT troops and Morgaine's men[235]. Even Lethbridge-Stewart is wise enough to hope to 'avoid bloodshed', though his suggested price for this is Morgaine's surrender.

More interesting, perhaps, is how this stance relates to the wider context of **Doctor Who**, during the Cartmel era as well as beyond it. From its beginnings to the present day, **Doctor Who** has always shown a deep ambivalence in its attitude towards the military, war

---

[234] Episode 1.
[235] Episodes 1, 3.

and conflict generally. While the Doctor is consistently a cerebral character who prefers to think their way out of a problem rather than using violence, the series deals in problems of a kind that can rarely be solved without some violence befalling somebody, and frequently either the Doctor or their associates are called on to mete it out. In the 21st century, the War Doctor's active participation in the Time War has been presented as an anomaly so extreme that he no longer warrants the name of 'the Doctor'[236], but the 13th Doctor's conflict-averse first season, from which many of her antagonists emerge entirely unscathed (to the point of one of them simply walking away unchallenged[237]), is equally aberrant.

Prior to 1989, the Doctor had been similarly inconsistent, but had moved over the series' quarter-century history towards the kind of rhetorical rejection of violence expressed in *Battlefield*. During the 1960s the Doctor had occasionally urged a culture to abandon its pacifist principles[238], or cheerfully sent an alien fleet hurtling into the sun[239]; but by the 1980s, when a story took a clear stance on armed conflict it would probably be a negative one[240], and it was accepted that genocide was, if not actually out of character for the Doctor, then at least something he would feel guilty about for a while afterwards[241].

---

[236] *The Name of the Doctor* (2013).
[237] *Arachnids in the UK* (2018).
[238] *The Daleks* (1963-64), *The Dominators* (1968).
[239] *The Seeds of Death* (1968).
[240] See, for instance, *The Awakening* (1984) or *Delta and the Bannermen* (1987).
[241] *Warriors of the Deep*, 'Terror of the Vervoids' (*The Trial of a Time Lord* episodes 9 to 12).

The seventh Doctor exhibits this dichotomy particularly starkly. He is generally averse to handling guns and contemptuous of those who rely on them, and he is almost suicidally inclined to talk his way out of dangerous situations. This is most clearly illustrated in his confrontation with the snipers in *The Happiness Patrol*: 'Why don't you do it, then? Look me in the eye, pull the trigger, end my life. Why not?'[242] When Mordred turns this rhetoric against him in *Battlefield* ('Come, then. Look me in the eye. End my life.'), the Doctor, like the snipers, demonstrates his humanity by not doing so, but Mordred's subsequent observation that 'It is a weakness, this lack of spirit,' mischaracterises this Doctor[243].

As ever, a reading of *Battlefield* is illuminated by the precedent of its philosophical twin, and in *Remembrance of the Daleks* the Doctor uses this same gift of persuasion to provoke Davros into launching a weapon of mass destruction against his own imperial subjects, the Daleks. That story ends with Ace's question, 'We did good, didn't we?', met by a characteristically equivocating reply: 'Perhaps. Time will tell. It always does.'[244] One of the titles Morgaine claims in *Battlefield* episode 2 is 'the Sun-Killer', which equally describes the Doctor at the climax of *Remembrance*. The seventh Doctor may show contempt for those who rely on guns or indeed swords, but he is quite capable of wielding weapons when expediency suggests it, whether to destroy Skaro's star system or (as he intends, before Lethbridge-Stewart confiscates the silver bullets from him) to shoot the Destroyer. This might be complicated by pointing out that both the Daleks and the

---

[242] *The Happiness Patrol* episode 2.
[243] *Battlefield* episode 4.
[244] *Remembrance of the Daleks* episode 4.

Destroyer are weapons as well as people; but so, in the Doctor's hands, are the likes of Lethbridge-Stewart and Ace.

The Destroyer acts as a metaphor for the other ultimate weapon in this story, the nuclear missile, which (at least as intended in the early story treatments) could destroy all life on Earth as the Hand of Omega destroyed life on Skaro. *Battlefield* ends with an inversion of the climactic scene of *Remembrance*, as the Doctor uses words alone to dissuade the story's villain from activating a devastating weapon. As he graphically describes the effects of such an annihilation, we might indeed suppose him to be guiltily recalling his own culpability for the Daleks' genocide[245].

Since both Aaronovitch and Cartmel were supporters of nuclear disarmament, it is possible that either may have intended this moment as a repudiation of the earlier story's genocidal resolution – perhaps even a moment of repentance or atonement that would inform the Doctor's future character and behaviour, such as his declaration in *Survival* that 'If we fight like animals, we die like animals!'[246] Perhaps an early-90s eighth Doctor under Cartmel would have been as much of a pacifist as Jodie Whittaker's 13th. A rejection of violent solutions such as single combat would at least explain why Morgaine does not die like so many other **Doctor Who** villains, but is instead arrested by a legitimate authority, despite the potential logistical difficulties this entails.

---

[245] Aaronovitch's novelisation of *Remembrance* includes its own 'CND speech' moment in its description of Skaro's passing, as innocent animals die in terror alongside the Daleks (Aaronovitch, *Remembrance of the Daleks* p152).
[246] *Survival* episode 3.

It seems more likely, though, that the plots of future seasons would (as they eventually did) require a Doctor equally capable of weaponising others and wiping out entire species (as he arguably does, in fact, in *The Curse of Fenric*). It seems more likely that this second pole of his personality asserts itself in *Battlefield* as a necessary corrective to that seen in *Remembrance*, with the two continuing to be held in tension.

Though 1980s **Doctor Who**'s ostensible rejection of war may be ascribed in part to a general change in social attitudes, as well as the embracing of progressive politics on the part of the programme-makers, the crystallisation of the character's attitude to the military was an outcome of the original UNIT era. These stories created much dramatic conflict by contrasting the Doctor's search for cerebral solutions to world-threatening problems with the combative instincts of the UNIT soldiers – especially Lethbridge-Stewart, the Dr Watson to his Sherlock Holmes. Though both approaches were generally essential to the dramatic resolution to these stories, when the Doctor and UNIT parted company it was his storyline, and the philosophy thereby ascribed to him, that the series continued to follow. Nevertheless, the Doctor's continued reliance on soldierly assistance remains visible in many post-UNIT stories, notably those script-edited by Cartmel's immediate predecessor Eric Saward[247].

The seventh Doctor's observation in *Battlefield* that 'Among all the varied wonders of the universe there's nothing so firmly clamped shut as the military mind' is a return to the cutting remarks often

---

[247] See particularly Saward's own stories *Earthshock* (1982), *Resurrection of the Daleks* and *Revelation of the Daleks* (1985).

made by his prior persona[248]. However, the regular military characters of the UNIT era were treated as sympathetic audience identification figures, and the third Doctor's ill-temper with them was often presented as unreasonable. Habitually in **Doctor Who** the 'military mind' is presented as inflexible, partisan and lacking in imagination, but also as reliable, methodical and conscientious – virtues that the Doctor often noticeably lacks. Such a mindset can create villains, such as General Carrington in *The Ambassadors of Death* (1970) or Sergeant Paterson in *Survival*, but it can also inform heroes whose qualities complement those of the Doctor, Lethbridge-Stewart being the archetypal example.

All of Aaronovitch's **Doctor Who** stories, in whatever medium, draw particularly on this tradition of sympathetic soldier characters, and *Battlefield* invites us to identify with Alastair and Bambera as much as it does with Doris or Shou Yuing, as well as with more minor characters like Lavel and Husak in the scenes where they appear. Though surprisingly only two of the soldiers given lines are killed during the story, Lavel's death is shown to be horrific and pitiful, and even Morgaine's Knight Commander is granted a moment of human dignity as the camera lingers on his boyish corpse.

This does not mean that the series' standard criticisms of the military are confined to the Doctor: Ace refers to Alistair as 'Colonel

---

[248] *Battlefield* episode 1; cf. *The Silurians* (1970) episode 2, *Terror of the Autons* (1971) episode 4, *Day of the Daleks* episode 1, *Frontier in Space* (1973) episode 4.

Blimp'[249], and Doris accuses him of 'playing soldier'[250]. However, it does mean that such criticisms are placed in the context of a story largely driven by military conflict, in which more than half the characters, including several who are likeable or heroic, belong to mundane or otherworldly armies. The military's dominance of the narrative is illustrated by the fact that it is Lethbridge-Stewart who attends Morgaine's ceremony to honour Earth's war dead, rather than the Doctor or Ace, who might feel moved to point out the irony of doing so while planning a war which will increase their number. In experiencing it through Alistair's eyes, though, instead of any potential hypocrisy on Morgaine's part we see her sense of honour – another military virtue in which the Doctor has little interest, but which is fundamental to her character.

Many of the complexities of Morgaine's personality, and much of what makes her sympathetic as a villain, relate to her preoccupation with honour. As well as Earth's war dead, she respects the temporary truce with Lethbridge-Stewart which her memorial observation imposes on her, while still promising to kill him when they next meet. She is even at pains to make clear that as a fellow warrior she bears him no malice. She is capable, in the same scene, of torturing Lavel to death for information and of dutifully paying with a miracle for the beer Mordred has consumed. Where many of the villains of **Doctor Who** either lack an ethical system or revel in their own evil, it is clear that Morgaine has a conscience and follows moral rules, but that these are largely alien

---

[249] Special Edition. Blimp was a character created by the newspaper cartoonist David Low. His name has become a byword for a particularly British strain of jingoistic, reactionary conservatism.
[250] *Battlefield* episode 1.

to our contemporary Western mindset[251]. (They are not, on the other hand, very similar to the code of medieval chivalry as practised in most traditional versions of Arthurian legend. Those would certainly discourage the mistreatment of a captured foe, and would frown even more sternly on summoning demons to victimise young women.)

From Mordred's taunting of Ancelyn as 'the Craven' we might assume that courage is an important element in this value system, and certainly Morgaine reacts angrily when her bravery is questioned, first by the Destroyer ('She fears me') and then by the Doctor ('Who do you fear more?')[252]. Indeed, she appears to release the Destroyer largely because the Doctor has reminded her of the demon's earlier taunts. If so, it is the only time she displays any weakness not connected with her son or her erstwhile lover.

The word 'honour' and its derivatives 'dishonoured' and 'honourable' are spoken eight times in the broadcast version of *Battlefield*, five times by Morgaine and once each by Ancelyn, Bambera and the Doctor. The Special Edition adds three more, one uttered by Lethbridge-Stewart and two by the Knight Commander. (For comparison, no such terms appear in Aaronovitch's *Remembrance*, or elsewhere in the 1989 season except once in the stock phrase 'guest of honour'[253].) Lethbridge-Stewart's allusion is

---

[251] Based both on Dave Owen's 'What If?' / '27 Up' and on the **Lost Stories** releases *Crime of the Century* and *Earth Aid*, a recurring enemy in the projected next season of **Doctor Who** would have been the Metatraxi, an alien species comically hampered by an even more eccentric sense of personal honour.
[252] Episode 4.
[253] *Ghost Light* episode 3.

to the military respect with which Lavel is to be buried, while Bambera and the Doctor both use it to convince denizens of the other world (specifically Ancelyn and Morgaine) to particular courses of action (running away and not setting off a nuclear holocaust, respectively). Despite his bragging, Ancelyn never uses the term of himself, instead with no special emphasis offering Lethbridge-Stewart 'the honour' of restoring Excalibur to its proper place[254].

Morgaine's and her Commander's uses of the term seem more significant. They make it clear that their cultural ideas of honour are closely tied to death. Mordred has 'dishonoured' Morgaine by failing to respect Earth's war dead, and as she observes, 'What is victory without honour?'[255] It seems of paramount importance that death in battle itself be 'honourable', both for the slayer and the slain. For Arthur to meet Morgaine in single combat would also show 'honour'. Morgaine is content to die provided it is 'with honour' (and appears to extend the same consideration to Mordred, assuming that this is what she has in mind when refusing to save him with the words 'Die well, my son.') The Knight Commander considers that, in killing their enemies with swords rather than guns, his men will both 'Make honour **our** standard' and 'Do **them** honour' (emphasis mine). And judging by Morgaine's final decision (in response to the Doctor's 'Is this honour? Is this war?'), she would see killing by nuclear missile as even less honourable than using firearms[256]. This is a point where Morgaine's morality system evidently coincides with the Doctor's, and

---

[254] *Battlefield* episodes 3, 4.
[255] Episode 2.
[256] Episode 4.

ultimately with that of the story itself – whose overall thrust is that war may be barbaric in general, but that nuclear war is despicable even by the standards of career warriors.

One candidate for the opposite of 'honour' is 'shame' – a word that is uttered only three times in *Battlefield*, on every occasion by Winifred Bambera. Its meaning in the script is not immediately obvious, but it clearly goes beyond its conventional British English usage as an expression of sympathy. Cartmel calls it 'a sort of all-purpose exclamation,' adding that Angela Bruce 'doesn't know what to make of the epithet'[257]. The first time she says it, in response to seeing the plight of two hitchhikers, Bambera appears to be using it in its familiar British English sense as an expression of sympathy (though sarcastically so, given her abrasive personality). The second time, as a reaction to seeing the TARDIS immediately after being told to look out for it, it has an odd neutral intonation, as if Bruce is indeed unsure of how it applies in this context. On the third occasion, on discovering that the tyre of her Range Rover has been punctured in a gun-battle, her delivery makes it sound, as some commentators have observed, very much like euphemistic swearing[258].

Cartmel quotes Aaronovitch as explaining that the word is 'something a West Indian would say'[259], implying that Aaronovitch intended Bambera's heritage to be Afro-Caribbean. I have been unable to confirm its usage in Caribbean English, but –

---

[257] Cartmel, *Script Doctor*, p154.
[258] E.g. Wood, *About Time 6* p291. All three instances are in episode 1.
[259] Cartmel, *Script Doctor*, p154.

121

interestingly, given the Special Edition's mention of 'Azania' and Bruce's view that this was important for Bambera's characterisation – the exclamation is used in South African English as a widely-applicable expression of surprise or pleasure[260]. Though it falls flat in the episode as filmed, Aaronovitch's choice of this rather obscure catchphrase for the consort-to-be of the Knight-General of the Britons may indeed be a bathetic counterpoint to the emphasis that Ancelyn's civilisation seems to place on honour.

---

[260] *Oxford English Dictionary*. On the face of it this may sound unlikely, but I have South African relatives who use it in precisely this way.

CHAPTER 7: 'SUFFICIENTLY ADVANCED MAGIC'

One innovation of the Cartmel era is relatively rarely remarked upon, compared with his more visible influence on the series' politics and dramatic techniques: 1988 and 1989 were the years when magic was most a part of **Doctor Who**.

The 1960s had seen two stories, *The Celestial Toymaker* (1966) and *The Mind Robber*, which would be better categorised as fantasy than as science fiction, although in the latter the manifestations of characters and tropes from fiction and myth are nebulously attributed to the intervention of an extraterrestrial computer rather than that of a bored godling. In the original UNIT era, the rule was that such eruptions of the fantastical were always justified as science, though in fact the explanations were little more than pseudoscientific technobabble. *The Dæmons* treats the question at length, though with little variation, as the Doctor answers Miss Hawthorne's assertions that Azal and his followers are committing acts of black magic with his own counter-assertions that they are actually explicable by recourse to such alien 'sciences' as psionics and matter conversion. Matt Barber's **Black Archive** volume on *The Dæmons* notes *The Brain of Morbius* (1976) and *Image of the Fendahl* (1977) as other stories that depict stereotypical witches with apparently magical powers that are ultimately explained by 'science', and argues that:

> 'From Old Mother, the doomed wise-woman in *An Unearthly Child* [...] to the Carrionites in *The Shakespeare Code* (2007), witches and witch-like characters in **Doctor Who** have been superficially powerful but, in the end, are

shown to be secondary to the rationality and science of the Doctor and his companions.'[261]

Similarly, in *The Day of the Daleks* and *The Time Warrior*, ghosts prove to be time-travellers from other eras; and in *The Time Monster* what appears to be the Titan Kronos is actually a life-form from the Time Vortex given the scientific-sounding descriptor 'Chronovore'. With occasional arguable exceptions like *State of Decay* (1980) – where vampires with seemingly supernatural characteristics are the acolytes of an alien (but perhaps equally supernatural) race – this convention became the norm throughout the 1970s and most of the 1980s. It is largely followed in 21st-century **Doctor Who** also, with entities such as ghosts, sirens and even Santa Claus being given relatively rational explanations for their existences[262] – although *The Impossible Planet / The Satan Pit* derives much of its drama and horror from apparently breaking this rule.

Cartmel's innovation was to partially remove this conceptual safety net. In his stories, gods are gods and magic is magic. Werewolves may be aliens and vampires mutated posthumans[263], but Lady Peinforte travels through time using 'Black magic, mostly', and the Gods of Ragnarok are never identified as anything but what their

---

[261] Barber, Matt, *The Black Archive #26: The Dæmons*, pp43-44.

[262] In *Army of Ghosts* (2006) and also *Hide* (2013), in *The Curse of the Black Spot* (2011) and in *Last Christmas* (2014), respectively.

[263] Mags in *The Greatest Show in the Galaxy* and the Haemovores in *The Curse of Fenric*. The Cheetah People of *Survival* are also reminiscent of folkloric were-animals, and like Mags they hail from another planet.

name suggests[264]. Light and Fenric give every appearance of being an angel and a djinn (albeit one given a name from Norse myth), and while their backgrounds are given complexities which suggest science-fiction wrinkles, both are ultimately shrugged away as evil entities from the beginning of time[265]. In being (as far as we are told) a 'demon' from 'Hell', the Destroyer takes this transgression against the norms of **Doctor Who** only slightly further, and yet he becomes perhaps the clearest expression of this particular Cartmelian trend.

Similarly, Morgaine is explicitly a 'sorceress' who deals in 'enchantments' and 'magic words'[266]. She, like Lady Peinforte, is a witch whose worldview, while contrasted with the Doctor's rationality, is never undercut by it and seems to coexist with equal validity (though their moral codes certainly come into conflict with the Doctor's). In the broadcast story, the basis of Morgaine's power is never questioned, and though the exchange regarding Clarke's Law in the Special Edition might have acted as a fig-leaf for this, it in fact makes it clear that the Doctor believes Arthur's world uses

---

[264] *Silver Nemesis* episode 1; *The Greatest Show in the Galaxy* episode 4.

[265] Fenric is said to be a 'force' of 'pure evil' from 'the dawn of time', the only sop to rationality being that the Doctor describes the beginning of time in terms that recall the Big Bang (*The Curse of Fenric* episode 3). And while we do learn that Light's angelic form is 'just its shape here on Earth', and that it has a spaceship, the Doctor's eventual conclusion is that it is 'an evil older than time itself' (*Ghost Light* episode 3).

[266] *Battlefield* episodes 2 to 4.

'advanced magic', not advanced technology[267]. As Merlin, the Doctor is the character in the story other than Morgaine who is most prominently associated with magical powers, and yet he has consistently claimed to work through technology: the most we see him do with magic in *Battlefield* is to protect against it with a simple chalk circle[268].

Morgaine's appears to be a world that has blended these two understandings into one – where they are, in fact, 'indistinguishable'. This seems to underlie (at a couple of removes mediated by the director's budget and the BBC design department) the presentation of all their artefacts except their relatively mundane guns and grenades. Although their world is repeatedly referred to as another 'dimension' or 'universe', and such locations can be accessed through technology in other **Doctor Who** stories[269], the method Mordred uses to summon Morgaine is, if not necessarily magical, at least highly ritualistic, and the props which accompany his words and gestures (two glowing orbs and a sword

---

[267] Morgaine's line 'Let us show them the limitations of their technologies' (episode 2) is of little help here, as it is unclear whether the limitations she speaks of apply to all technology, or merely to near-future Earth's.

[268] Cartmel's first **New Adventure**, *Cat's Cradle: Warhead* (1992), would suggest that the scientific and the magical are merely alternative paradigms by which the Doctor's nature and experiences can be understood – though clearly the weight of **Doctor Who** continuity is with the former (Cartmel, Andrew, *Cat's Cradle: Warhead*, pp183-86).

[269] Notably in *Inferno* and *Full Circle* (1980), but also, according to the standard explanation for its oversized interior, every time anybody walks into or out of the TARDIS.

that matches Excalibur) could be read equally as belonging to either paradigm. Even the Destroyer's death by silver bullet (a traditional method in folklore for dispatching werewolves) blends an alchemical belief in the purity of silver with the technological delivery system of Lethbridge-Stewart's sidearm[270].

Morgaine is the focus of all the magic in the story. The only other characters we see actively using it are Mordred (who is summoning her at the time) and the Destroyer (who is summoned by her). We are, though, given very little insight into how it works, or where her abilities come from, unless it be the oblique references to her 'Fay' affiliations. In Ben Aaronovitch's **Rivers of London** books – as in most good works of literary fantasy where wizardry plays a significant part – there is a carefully thought-through magical system which underlies the structure of the spells, limits what practitioners can accomplish, and ensures that any achievement of worth exacts a cost from the achiever. On the face of it, Morgaine's abilities are much more simplistically conceived: whatever she wants, she can do by enchantment. Influencing the minds of scared teenagers, restoring a blind woman's sight, shooting down a helicopter with lightning and summoning a demon from Hell all appear to come equally easily to her. The only act of sorcery which seems to cause anybody any effort or sense of accomplishment is Mordred's establishing of the dimensional gateway, and this may be purely because he is less blasé about working spells than she is. (His evident sense of triumph is particularly odd in that all he must

---

[270] It also recalls Ace's dispatching of a Cyberman using a catapult loaded with a gold coin in *Silver Nemesis*.

surely have passed through such a portal already to be on Earth at all.)

Still, Morgaine pays a price in the end: she loses Arthur. While there is little to suggest that her individual acts of sorcery have cost her anything, her wholesale adoption of witchery has lost her the love of her life. By acquiring power through supernatural means, she has, figuratively speaking, lost her soul, and in that respect her fate is that of that archetypal magician, Faust[271]. Even so, it is one that many another **Doctor Who** villain has achieved in a magic-free universe, by allying themselves with the Dæmons, the Osirians, the Daleks, or any other alien menace that promises much and delivers nothing.

---

[271] In German legend and various literary adaptations, Faust sells his soul to the Devil in exchange for worldly knowledge, wealth and power, but is unable to connive, buy or threaten his way out of being dragged down to Hell when his bargain comes to an end. See Barber, *The Dæmons*, for more on Faust, science vs magic, and Clarke's Third Law.

CHAPTER 8: BRITISHNESS, AND OTHER IDENTITIES

When Ace refers to Arthur as 'King of the Britons', as she does several times[272], she is perhaps thinking of *Monty Python and the Holy Grail*, where Graham Chapman's Arthur repeatedly introduces himself in this way. The use of the ethnonym is apparently confirmed, however, by Ancelyn calling himself 'Knight-General of the Britons,' and referring to 'The time when Arthur rises to lead the Britons to war.'[273]

Though the name is used generically in a modern context to mean all citizens of the United Kingdom, in the Arthurian mythos the 'Britons' are specifically the Romano-Celtic inhabitants of Great Britain and Brittany in the early first millennium, who Arthur defends (ultimately unsuccessfully, even according to the legends) from the invading Saxons. As we have already seen, Aaronovitch's story treatments and draft scripts referred to the 'Br'tons' and 'S'rax', a formulation which survives only in Morgaine's claim to be the 'Battle-Queen' of the latter, but an echo of this ancient ethnic conflict seemingly underlies the backstory of the opposing sides in the drama, as Aaronovitch originally conceived them.

That Ancelyn's people call themselves 'Britons' despite apparently originating in an entirely different dimension from the people we know by that name is intriguing, but as there was evidently interaction between the two universes in ancient times its precise significance is not clear. More interesting in the light of *Battlefield*'s

---

[272] Twice in episode 2 and once more in the Special Edition.
[273] Episodes 2 and 1 respectively.

philosophical pairing with *Remembrance of the Daleks* are the political overtones that the prophecy of Arthur's militant return, identified by Ancelyn as 'The time of restitution', takes on in this context[274]. While the Arthurian myths have rarely been used by British fascists of the kind *Remembrance* depicts, myths about the restoration of a nation's imaginary glorious, often chivalric, past are frequently co-opted by ethnonationalist movements generally. When Shou Yuing suggests that 'it's not my mythology,' she is echoing the views of white Britons (in the modern sense, there being none in the ancient sense left) who would deny her any ownership of Britain's cultural heritage[275]. It seems unlikely that this possible response to the myth would be lost on Aaronovitch, coming as he did from a family of Jewish Marxist immigrants[276], and this may be another reason, aside from narrative convenience, for *Battlefield* eventually to disown the prophecy as 'propaganda'[277].

I have noted in discussing the diversity of *Battlefield*'s cast that – although Husak is the only earthly character whose nationality is explicitly referenced – he and the foreign-accented characters working for an international organisation, Lavel and Zbrigniev, are all white Europeans, while so far as we know the ethnic minority characters, Bambera and Shou Yuing, are both British. Although in the first story treatment Bambera is a USAF officer, so would presumably have been American, this aspect of her character is lost

---

[274] Episode 2.
[275] Episode 3.
[276] Grahl, John, 'Obituary: Sam Aaronovitch', *The Independent*, 8 June 1998.
[277] Episode 4.

in later drafts, and Angela Bruce is British (of West Indian and white British parentage) and plays the part as such. Though Shou Yuing's name ('Thai' in the first story treatment) has always suggested an East Asian heritage, both the preliminary story drafts indicate that she is a student who is 'back home for the holidays', and she is on first-name terms with Peter Warmsly and Pat Rowlinson, which taken together strongly suggest her family are local residents[278]. While she may deny interest in the Arthurian myths, she also associates them with Warmsly (who she says has 'got this thing about King Arthur') and his dig, to which her attitude is an ambivalent one – she tells Ace 'Can't see it myself, all that patient scraping about,' but we later learn that she has in fact been helping Warmsly with his work there[279]. We never learn what she might consider 'my mythology' to be.

Other than when Ace is under Morgaine's influence, the only instance of xenophobia in the story is when Pat Rowlinson asks Husak, irrelevantly and in a somewhat hostile tone, 'You're not English, are you?' Pat knows Shou Yuing and has met Bambera, and has shown no sign of prejudice towards either of them[280]. Though he is under stress at this point, bewildered by his wife's miraculous healing and resenting the local population's evacuation, the implication is that he may have nationalistic prejudices but not racist ones. His specific choice of wording ('English' rather than 'British') might even suggest something about future relations between the nations of the United Kingdom, but is more likely to

---

[278] BBC WAC T65/271/1, 12 and 20 September 1988, episode 2.
[279] Episodes 2 and 3.
[280] Admittedly, Shou Yuing is his paying customer, and it would take a bold racist to disrespect Bambera to her face.

be a specific kind of verbal carelessness not uncommon among English people, like Ace's historically inauthentic, 'Here, you can be King of England'[281]. It would be optimistic to suppose that racism has been eliminated entirely in this near future – Shou Yuing's reaction to Ace's slurs is not baffled incomprehension – but the overall effect is to show British society as generally accepting of minority ethnicities, perhaps slightly at the expense of white foreigners.

As far as Ancelyn's world is concerned, despite his loyalty to the 'Britons' – and the fact that everyone we see from his dimension seems to be white – he apparently has no aversion to forming a relationship with Bambera. The Arthurian myths are in fact less ethnically homogeneous than is sometimes realised, including sympathetic 'Saracen' characters such as Sir Palamides, a knight of the Round Table who plays a significant part in the legend of Tristan and Isolde[282]. Indeed, if it is true that Ancelyn's opponents – the only other living people from his dimension we see – are S'rax rather than Britons, Ancelyn's own whiteness is no evidence that his people are not as ethnically varied as those of Bambera's Britain.

Though Aaronovitch's work, both in **Doctor Who** and outside it, is rooted in Britishness, it interprets that elusive quality broadly, and sees it in a context which is both wide and deep. Aaronovitch takes

---

[281] Episode 3. The name 'England' dates from the ninth century and refers specifically to the area eventually colonised by the Anglo-Saxons whose initial waves of invasion Arthur supposedly resisted.
[282] He appears extensively in Malory, initially in book VIII chapter 10.

a long view of history, depicting a present – or in the case of *Battlefield* and his **New Adventures**, a future – informed by aspects of the distant past (which in the case of the more distant futures may actually be the present). The history of London is a constant, haunting presence in the **Rivers of London** books, and 'Terra Incognita' – an intriguing fragment of a novel in Big Finish Productions' **Bernice Summerfield** series which Aaronovitch began, but seemingly never finished, at around the time *Rivers of London* found its first success[283] – takes a similar approach from a science-fiction angle, depicting a 26th-century London equally in debt to its heritage. The sole published chapter of 'Terra Incognita' calls London 'a city entirely composed of ethnic minorities', some of them by this time extraterrestrial, and this view – the geographical equivalent of his embracing of deep history – is also typical[284]. In the **Rivers of London** series, the adopted goddesses of the London waterways are all women of African descent, and the protagonist is a Metropolitan Police constable of white British and Sierra Leonean parentage[285].

Aaronovitch sees humanity, the British, and Londoners in particular, as heterogeneous and promiscuously hybridised as a product of their history, and it is this specific form of Britishness his

---

[283] The novel as a whole remains unpublished, and the most recent reference to it on Aaronovitch's blog is from April 2009, expressing the hope that it would be finished within two years (Aaronovitch, Ben, 'Back on the Menu').

[284] The chapter was published, as a 'teaser' for marketing purposes, in the 2007 **Bernice Summerfield** anthology *Missing Adventures* (ed Rebecca Levene). This quote is from *Missing Adventures* p233.

[285] This is the same heritage as gives rise to the African Lethbridge-Stewarts, Kadiatu's family, in Aaronovitch's **New Adventures**.

work as a whole passionately celebrates. Even the quintessential national hero King Arthur, in his hands, is reinvented as an immigrant of sorts – a 'Briton', but one who came here from another place entirely. In these terms, Arthur's prominence in British legend and history becomes another aspect of the pervasive influence of figures originally estranged in distance, time or both from Britain's here and now.

Within this context, the **Rivers of London** series foregrounds other aspects of British – and human – diversity, involving characters both sympathetic and unsympathetic of various faiths, sexualities and ethnicities, as well as inventing its own magical and supernatural minorities. Gender expectations are also subverted, and a large proportion of the characters are women, playing varied, substantial and important parts. While *Battlefield* is less adventurous – religion is largely absent, and **Doctor Who** in 1989 was not yet ready for the overt acknowledgement of non-heterosexual attraction that it would cheerfully make 16 years later – this celebration of human difference is recognisably present in the story's foreign, ethnic minority and female characters.

Though it falls short of gender parity in its cast[286], *Battlefield* comes closer than most **Doctor Who** stories of its decade, and scores even more highly over the 1970s UNIT stories it evokes, where not infrequently there would be only one non-regular female speaking character, generally in a subordinate role[287]. In fact, if one leaves aside the generally more liberated participation of the Doctor's

---

[286] By my count, it has seven credited female parts to 10 male.
[287] See, for instance, *Inferno, Terror of the Autons, The Three Doctors* (1972-73) and *Invasion of the Dinosaurs* (1974).

female companions, this period has a not dissimilar gender politics to the traditional Arthurian myths: the heroes and villains are usually men; most of the former, other than their mysterious and wise mentor, are soldiers who win honour by fighting; women appear as wives or romantic partners and as servants (or their modern equivalents – radio operators, lab technicians, administrative staff), and the most memorable of the exceptions is, literally, a witch[288]. It is not difficult to see how such a parallel would present itself to a writer seeking to use both these bodies of work as source material, nor why a progressive-minded writer like Aaronovitch would seek to update it – though clearly he goes less far than Moffat would in the 2010s, presenting in such stories as *Dark Water / Death in Heaven* (2014) and *The Magician's Apprentice* a 21st-century UNIT led by a female Lethbridge-Stewart, advised by a female scientific expert and fighting a female Master. As I have noted, however, in making **his** female Brigadier also a Guinevere figure – and thus reversing the passivity and conformity to traditional gender roles of the Guinevere of legend – Aaronovitch critiques not only the patriarchal assumptions of the 1970s UNIT stories but also those of Arthurian myth.

These feminist tendencies surface elsewhere in the story, with Ace's habitual angry defiance of authority making itself felt against Lethbridge-Stewart's paternalism, and inspiring a similar independence in Shou Yuing; in Lavel's bravery and her comradely banter with Lethbridge-Stewart; and even in Elizabeth Rowlinson's refusal of help as she is being evacuated. (Elizabeth could stand as a further example of diversity, given her disability, but this

---

[288] Miss Hawthorne in *The Dæmons*.

becomes questionable when she is cured of her blindness. That said, Morgaine asks for no permission before doing so, and we are not privy to Elizabeth's view of this violation of her autonomy.) It is true that, in pairing off his newly-introduced female Brigadier with a male guest character in the manner of companions like Susan and Leela, Aaronovitch perhaps treats her less progressively[289]; but he originally had sound thematic reasons for this; and *Battlefield* is, after all, the story which finally shows her predecessor as part of a domestic couple.

The final scene brings issues with it that are not confined to its startling change of tone from military thriller to whimsical domestic comedy. When Doris celebrates her husband's victory with a trip 'Out with the girls' (Ace, Shou Yuing, Bambera and arguably Bessie), leaving Alistair, Ancelyn and the Doctor to carry out various domestic chores, the feminist message is obvious. Clearly, the scene acts as payback for Alistair's earlier abandonment of Doris (whose forbearance during his absence is more visible in the rehearsal script); and in the longer view, for the scenes in early 70s **Doctor Who** where it was accepted that 'the girls' would make the tea, coffee and sandwiches for the benefit of men including Alistair and the Doctor[290]. (This tendency was, incidentally, critiqued in slightly later 70s stories[291], and has already been alluded to by Bambera after being asked by Alistair to provide a blanket for the

---

[289] A point made by, among others, Fiona Moore (Moore, Fiona, 'You Mean All This Time We Could Have Been Friends?').

[290] See, for instance, *Spearhead from Space* episode 1 (1971), *The Sea Devils* episode 4 and *The Time Monster* episode 1.

[291] Jo Grant, who is most often at its receiving end, complains of it in both *Frontier in Space* episode 4 and *The Green Death* episode 4.

lake-soaked Ace[292].) It is equally true that the restatement of the domestic is a necessary corrective to the tone of a narrative which has, as I have observed, been dominated by military concerns.

However, the statement made by the scene is so obvious as to be painfully didactic, and there is much about it that feels ill-judged. Doris has not interacted with any of the other women during the story, and the idea that their gender gives her more in common with them than with the three men is a dubious one. (We can be sure that Bambera in particular would place exactly the same priority on her military over her domestic duties as Alistair, and the fact that this would be a less conventional choice for a woman would make it neither a more nor a less ethical one.) Nor was Alistair's temporary absence a selfish one; while away he has been instrumental in saving the world (including Doris herself) from magical and nuclear annihilation. Although there is no question that the women have made contributions of similar weight, there is no obvious basis in the story to conclude that they deserve a celebration more than their male counterparts. It would not be entirely unreasonable for a viewer to feel that Alistair, Ancelyn and the Doctor were entitled to more consideration than the scene chooses to show them; and although the theme of Bambera's sovereignty over her own life is, as we have seen, justified by the Arthurian material, it compromises the narrative of the couple's burgeoning love to have her treating Ancelyn as a servant.

Though it is a feminist scene, in giving the viewer scope to judge Doris's feminist behaviour as unreasonable, Aaronovitch undercuts the point he presumably hopes to make. A less damaging and more

---

[292] Special Edition.

natural conclusion (of the sort we might expect from the 21st-century series) would have portrayed all seven characters partying together, without such a distinction being made between them, much as Lavel has earlier been seen working with Alistair without her gender being an issue[293]. The scene makes for a suitably awkward culmination of a story which has throughout been passionate about feminism, but also rather unsure of what to do about it – a story whose powerful, strongly characterised female villain is also an indulgent mother ultimately motivated by her longing for a particular man. While *Battlefield* makes a fine job of celebrating the rich diversity of British cultural identity, in the case of female identity its good intentions are perhaps less well rewarded with success.

---

[293] As Moore observes, 'The message of post-millennial **Doctor Who** is clear: you can have friendships and professional relationships with people of all genders' ('You Mean All This Time We Could Have Been Friends?').

CHAPTER 9: 'IT'S ONLY A TRAP'

Etymological considerations aside, there is valid reason for *Battlefield* to downplay the idea, emphasised in both the story treatments, that Winifred Bambera is predisposed by her given name to fall in love with the nearest equivalent to Queen Guinevere's lover Sir Lancelot[294].

As we have seen, in *Battlefield* there are three characters – the Doctor, Morgaine and Mordred – who are explicitly the same people as figures in Arthurian myth, while others, primarily Lethbridge-Stewart and Ace, play analogous roles without it being suggested that this is an intrinsic part of who they are. (Both had, after all, appeared in other **Doctor Who** stories – in Lethbridge-Stewart's case a great many of them – without attracting any such symbolism.) Ancelyn and Bambera fall between these two categories, as original characters of Aaronovitch's whose destiny is nevertheless, it is suggested, dictated by the structures of a myth – though in *Battlefield*'s terms it is a history – well over a millennium old.

Ancelyn at least comes from a culture which might be expected to accept this sort of idea, given the prominence of prophecy, destiny and divine providence in the Arthurian corpus, but such a circumscribed fate seems harsh on Bambera, who is in other respects a modern, independent woman admirable for her firmness and force of personality.

In this context, the fact that the romance is written and played so unconvincingly is unfortunate. Marcus Gilbert depicts Ancelyn's

---

[294] BBC WAC T65/271/1, 12 and 20 September 1988.

love for Winifred with the same naïve earnestness as the other aspects of his personality, and Angela Bruce varies Bambera's blunt gruffness very little depending on her emotional context. Though a different director might have fruitfully played up this contrast for comedic purposes, Bambera's impassiveness instead gives the impression that forming a relationship with Ancelyn, like escorting the nuclear missile, is an irksome duty which she is nonetheless obliged to perform.

Although very little attention is drawn to it in the broadcast version of the story, the idea that Bambera's name influences or explains her behaviour persists in the Doctor's enigmatic comment about the 'many secrets in names'[295]. The other characters allow this to pass without further inquiry, but the viewer seeking to understand it is pointed towards Aaronovitch's original intentions by multiple sources[296]. The effect this has on our perception of Bambera's autonomy is damaging, compromising the idea of her sovereignty over her own life in favour of making her emotions subject to the dictates of some ill-defined authority.

There are several possible explanations for the affinity that Bambera and Ancelyn evidently have with Guinevere and Lancelot, none of them supported in the story and none of them ultimately

---

[295] *Battlefield* episode 1. Note that the Doctor says this considerably before Bambera or anyone else is introduced to Ancelyn, and that the story requires him to have little knowledge of what is to follow. He must at this stage be responding to the name in the context of a general Arthurian ambiance, rather than making any specific predictions of its likely significance.
[296] See Platt, *Battlefield* p74; Cartmel, *Script Doctor* p154; Pixley, 'The DWM Archive: *Battlefield*' p29.

convincing. Perhaps the least troubling would be that Bambera is displaying 'nominative determinism', the (not always seriously) proposed phenomenon that impels some people into professions or roles in life which correspond to their names[297]. By this reading, Bambera would have learned at some point that her given name derived from Guinevere's, and would be subconsciously seeking out a Lancelot to fall in love with. This may sound out of character for Bambera, but it at least makes her to some extent the author of her own fate.

Platt's novelisation, ignoring the implications of 'ap Gwalchmai', suggests that Ancelyn is Lancelot's descendant[298]. However, there is little scope in the traditional Arthurian myth for Winifred to be Guinevere's[299]; and even if she was, some further explanation for her behaviour would surely be needed, as most of us manage to go through life without, as far as we know, mimicking the emotional responses of specific Dark Ages ancestors. The stronger idea that Ancelyn and Bambera behave as they do because they are reincarnations of the original Lancelot and Guinevere might be seen as unlikely in view of the general Christian metaphysics of the Arthurian mythos – not to mention the overall rationalism of

---

[297] Popular examples include the neurologist Lord Brain (1895-1966) and Lord Chief Justice Judge (1941-).

[298] He is 'doubtless' Lancelot's descendant, sharing his family home of Garde-Joyeuse and claiming distant descent from Sir Galahad, traditionally his son (Platt, *Battlefield* pp36, 65, 74, 171).

[299] Lacey notes that 'All the English chronicles comment on the misfortune of [Guinevere's] barrenness as Arthur's wife.' He does add that 'Welsh tradition maintained that she bore him sons,' which perhaps leaves a slim possibility that Bambera is a descendant of Guinevere **and of Arthur** (Lacey, p262).

Doctor Who, despite its occasional flirtations with Buddhism – but it has been a fairly frequent plot device in stories which place Arthurian characters in a modern or futuristic setting, including Barr and Bolland's *Camelot 3000*[300].

In Bambera's case, though, her personality is so different from that normally ascribed to Arthur's queen that it is difficult to see what such a 'reincarnation' would actually mean, unless it was that the same legends which apparently faithfully depicted Guinevere's love for Lancelot, and have proven a good guide to Morgaine's and Mordred's characters, were radically wrong about all other aspects of hers. (Interestingly, her personality – and hairstyle – are a reasonable match for those of *Camelot 3000*'s Sir Tristan, who is reincarnated as a woman and can only resume the legendary affair with Isolde in a sapphic capacity. Though possibly verging on a lesbian stereotype, this Tristan's macho self-assertion and stubborn reluctance to accede to the inevitable are unusual qualities to see in a female character of the era, and not enormously different from how Bambera is presented.)

An equally dubious suggestion might be that some external force – a by-product of Excalibur's presence, perhaps – is inducing those present to act out stories recapitulating those of the Arthurian

---

[300] Other instances include the Australian TV series **Guinevere Jones** (2002), as well as numerous fantasy novels, including examples by Peter David and Guy Gavriel Kay. (David also wrote a bafflingly incompatible sequel to *Battlefield*, 'One Fateful Knight', in the Big Finish short story anthology *Short Trips: The Quality of Leadership*.)

myths[301], but the fact that Bambera and Ancelyn's affair is apparently serenely unimpeded by any barriers that might give rise to betrayal, tragic separation and death, makes this seem unlikely, or at least strangely selective. Beyond this, we are left with the possibility of a pseudo-divine plan (possibly one of Merlin's) in which the couple's union serves a purpose outside the scope of the story itself, and the names they have been given are merely a hint nudging them towards this destiny.

However talkative Aaronovitch may have been about wanting his story to involve a romance between a new Guinevere and a new Lancelot, his actual reasons are opaque and may be purely aesthetic. The higher power that ordains Bambera's lot is simply Aaronovitch's authorial fiat – she is, in fact, constrained as much by her own role in *Battlefield* as by Guinevere's in *Le Morte D'Arthur*.

When other **Doctor Who** stories have toyed with the idea of predestined behaviour based on naming or ancestry, as in *Image of the Fendahl* and *Battlefield*'s close successor *The Curse of Fenric*, this is treated as a source of horror, an infringement of the personal identity and freedom of will which are valued so highly in **Doctor Who**'s humanistic worldview. In *Battlefield* the intention is apparently more benign, but the effect when this background is known is to radically undercut Bambera's autonomy and thus to compromise the feminist critique of the Arthurian patriarchy and that of UNIT-era **Doctor Who** which she otherwise expresses.

---

[301] A parallel might be found in Alan Garner's novel *The Owl Service* (1967), hauntingly adapted for TV in 1969-70, where a different love triangle, from the Welsh legend of Blodeuwedd and Lleu, is much more savagely recapitulated.

Fortunately, by avoiding explicitly commenting on this, the broadcast story is able to maintain this function of hers very nearly intact.

However, Bambera is not the only character in the grip of an inescapable fate over which she has no control. The Doctor, as we have learned by the end of the story, will become the Merlin remembered by Morgaine, Mordred and (by repute, at least) Ancelyn, and much of his future life is mapped out in the knowledge they reveal. We know that he will leave various hints and exploits for his past self, including a marker for the tunnel to the drowned spaceship, a door keyed to his voice pattern and a note explaining about Arthur's demise. We know that he will lose to Morgaine at chess, that he will cast her down at Badon 'with his mighty arts', and that she will eventually seal him 'into the ice caves for all eternity'[302]. To the extent that the accounts of Malory and others may be true, we may indeed be able to deduce a great deal more than this.

At this point in the history of **Doctor Who**, hints of the Doctor's unwritten future were rare, and never fulfilled in the long term. A story like *The Two Doctors* (1985), where the sixth Doctor teamed up with an earlier counterpart, would have been impossible to pull off in reverse, thanks to the impracticality of predicting or binding the choices of future production teams. When Michael Jayston appeared in *The Trial of a Time Lord* as the Valeyard, a distillation of the Doctor's worst nature who is ambiguously also his future self, there was no serious expectation that Jayston would therefore one day be cast as the series' regular protagonist. Decades later,

---

[302] Episodes 2, 4.

the titular character in Russell T Davies' script *The Next Doctor* (2008) would turn out not to be, and while Steven Moffat's stewardship of the series would allow him to follow up *Silence in the Library / Forest of the Dead* (2008) in a way which had not been attempted before, at the time of broadcast there was no more reason to imagine that the viewer would see the Doctor become River Song's husband than there had been to suppose that they would see him become the Valeyard or Merlin.

Battlefield is ingenious in not showing us its future Doctor: we are told only that he has a different face from Sylvester McCoy's, and Morgaine knows that he has had many[303]. If villains like Sil and the Rani, and ambiguous allies like Lytton and Glitz, could return a year or two after their first appearances[304], then it was perhaps plausible that Marsh, at least, could have reappeared as a younger Morgaine alongside McCoy's successor in a 1990 or 1991 season[305]. Such a prequel would probably not have resulted in the Doctor being permanently imprisoned in Morgaine's ice caves; but the threat of the series' cancellation was unrelenting from the mid-1980s, and the production team had responded to it before by

---

[303] Episode 2.

[304] Sil appears in *Vengeance on Varos* (1985) and 'Mindwarp' (*The Trial of a Time Lord* episodes 5 to 8); the Rani in *The Mark of the Rani* (1985) and *Time and the Rani*; Lytton in *Resurrection of the Daleks* and *Attack of the Cybermen* (1985); Glitz in 'The Mysterious Planet' and 'The Ultimate Foe' (*The Trial of a Time Lord* episodes 1 to 4 and 13 to 14) and *Dragonfire*.

[305] No such intention appears to have existed, judging by Owen's 'What If?' / '27 Up' and his later comment that Cartmel 'definitely never mentioned bringing back [...] characters from his watch,' but in terms of audience perception the point remains.

flirting with an apparently final ending, so it is perhaps not altogether out of the question[306]. In practical terms, though, it must be admitted that even in 1989 it was unlikely that the full backstory of *Battlefield* would ever be explored in the future of **Doctor Who** – if indeed it had one.

For *Battlefield*'s own purposes, however, the Doctor faces revelations about his future which may include news of his eventual doom, and he accepts the prospect with remarkable equanimity – indeed, he seems positively blasé about it, although it is one of the first things he learns about 'Merlin', early in episode 2. Perhaps this is because he is convinced he can escape from any ice cave (and any putative prequel story would more likely have shown him making a clever getaway while contriving for Morgaine to believe that he remained imprisoned); or perhaps he believes that as a time-traveller he has the option to change his own future (and clearly he does not from this point act as if his survival until he can visit the past of an alternative Britain is an unshakeable certainty). Most likely, though, it is because the Doctor's habitual response to threats, however ominous or unavoidable, is to scoff in their faces and focus on immediate practicalities.

Before he was known as a wizard, the Merlin of the Celtic tradition was a prophet, and knowledge of the future was his stock-in-trade[307]; as I have discussed, it is easy to see how a memory of *Battlefield*, combined with a sound knowledge of Malory, would

---

[306] See Cooray Smith, James, *The Black Archive 14: The Ultimate Foe* for the appearance of a similar idea in early drafts of *The Trial of a Time Lord* episode 14.

[307] Lacey pp383-83.

146

stand a future Doctor in good stead in this role. The most famous prophecy in the Arthurian mythos, however – that of Arthur's return at the time of Britain's greatest need – is explicitly dismissed in *Battlefield* as 'propaganda'[308]. In this case, it is Arthur who has a predetermined role in the story – to rise, as he did in Aaronovitch's early story treatments, and act as a deus ex machina to resolve the nation's wrongs in general and the story's conflicts in particular – and it is one he escapes, admittedly through the inconvenient method of dying first.

We might see Lethbridge-Stewart's survival of his showdown with the Destroyer in the same metatextual light. He, too, had a particular role in Aaronovitch's story treatments, and the structure of the story requires him to fulfil it by dying; yet he escapes this fate and lives. Equally, while the Doctor's foreknowledge requires his friend to die in bed, the future Merlin considers it perfectly plausible in the aftermath of the confrontation that he has confounded this prophecy by dying early and heroically. Apparently, neither the demands of narrative nor the Doctor's memories of the historical record can constrain Lethbridge-Stewart; he makes his own fate. And if this is true of the Brigadier, how much more so of the Doctor.

The application to Merlin's supposedly inescapable doom is clear: prophecies and destiny and divine providence are not worth the paper they are hastily scribbled on. If the Doctor, Lethbridge-

---

[308] It is clear that Merlin colluded in this at the very least, and probably started the legend himself. Given that even in *Battlefield* the Doctor remembers the existence of the prophecy, perhaps this too is something he is predestined to do.

Stewart and, less happily, Arthur, can hope to avoid their ordained fates, then it certainly makes sense for Aaronovitch to downplay Bambera's subjugation to hers. Her engagement to Ancelyn, if such it is, may well be a happy outcome for them both, but if so it should take place because they both choose it, not because her name is Winifred.

Again, as this aspect of the story becomes less prominent in successive drafts, we can see Aaronovitch progressing towards a completer understanding and control of his plot and themes; again though, and frustratingly, the final scripted version of *Battlefield* never quite reaches the endpoint which would have made them harmonise.

CONCLUSION

I spoke in the Introduction about the unforgiving consensus surrounding *Battlefield* in **Doctor Who** fandom. The most fundamental truth in **Doctor Who** fandom, however, is that no consensus is universal. From every widely-held opinion there are dissenters, and for everyone insisting that such-and-such a view is held by all true fans, there'll be another who'll swear that everyone **they** know thinks exactly the opposite. Doctors, companions, showrunners – all have devotees who will declare them superior to all others, and detractors who consider them undeniably the worst thing ever.

So too with individual stories: there's no **Doctor Who** episode or serial so beloved that no fan will disparage it, nor any so widely held in contempt that nobody will declare it their favourite.

There are, in all honesty, a great many **Doctor Who** stories that I'd put in the category 'Better than *Battlefield*', but for many years – 16, to be precise – it was my favourite story. The Arthurian themes chimed with another of my particular childhood enthusiasms, still present when I saw it on first broadcast at the age of 17; but also I loved the near-future setting, admired the pacifist message, and appreciated the revisionist approach to past continuity. Later, its obvious influence on the philosophy and aesthetic of the **New Adventures** novels that Aaronovitch and Cartmel helped shape, and which I followed avidly during my university years, cemented its place in my affections.

For a long time the catharsis of the climax, with the Doctor's horrific word-picture of a nuclear holocaust triggering Morgaine's anguished admission of defeat and then of her lost and unrequited love, would unfailingly make me teary. Until 2005, it was the only moment in **Doctor Who** that ever had.

I don't expect these subjective recollections to elevate *Battlefield* in anybody else's affections, let alone convince them of its merits. As I say, every **Doctor Who** story can claim to be somebody's favourite, even the ones we personally think are terrible. It may well be that the good aspects of *Battlefield* are insufficient to make it a good **Doctor Who** story. It may even be – frustratingly, because given its starting conditions it should have been a triumph – that in the final analysis, *Battlefield* is a bit of a mess. But it's also the programme's only intersection with one of the other defining myths of Britishness, whose piety, violent tendencies and authoritarian sympathies might have placed it very much at odds with **Doctor Who**'s own worldview; and it finds, in the identification of that wise, benevolent, dangerous magician the Doctor with Merlin, the perfect way to marry these two mythologies.

Sadly, the version of *Battlefield* that exists in my head will always be better than the version that exists in reality – but that, perhaps, is in the nature of myth. Perhaps, if there really are other universes, then somewhere there is a world where the reality of *Battlefield* comes closer to the imagination of it, and it really is the magnificent saga of heroic return and heartbreaking sacrifice it promised to be.

BIBLIOGRAPHY

Documents

BBC Written Archives Centre file T65/271/1.

Story treatment, 12 September 1988.

Story treatment, 20 September 1988.

Studio script changes, 11 May 1989.

Rehearsal script, undated.

Owen, Dave, private correspondence with author, 11 March 2018.

Books

Aaronovitch, Ben, *Remembrance of the Daleks*. **The Target Doctor Who Library** #148. London, Virgin Publishing, 1990. ISBN 9780426203377.

Aaronovitch, Ben, *Transit*. **Doctor Who: The New Adventures**. London, Virgin Publishing Ltd, 1992. ISBN 9780426203841.

Aaronovitch, Ben, *The Also People*. **Doctor Who: The New Adventures**. London, Virgin Publishing Ltd, 1995. ISBN 9780426204565.

Aaronovitch, Ben, *Rivers of London*. London, Gollancz, 2011. ISBN 9780575097568.

Aaronovitch, Ben, *Moon over Soho*. London, Gollancz, 2011. ISBN 9780575097605.

Aaronovitch, Ben, *Whispers under Ground*. London, Gollancz, 2012. ISBN 9780575097643.

Aaronovitch, Ben, *Broken Homes*. London, Gollancz, 2013. ISBN 9780575132467.

Aaronovitch, Ben, *Foxglove Summer*. London, Gollancz, 2014. ISBN 9780575132504.

Aaronovitch, Ben, *The Hanging Tree*. London, Gollancz, 2016. ISBN 9780575132559.

Aaronovitch, Ben, and Kate Orman, *So Vile a Sin*. **Doctor Who: The New Adventures**. London, Virgin Publishing Ltd, 1997. ISBN 9780426204848.

Barber, Matt, *The Black Archive #26: The Dæmons*. **The Black Archive** #26. Edinburgh, Obverse Books, 2018. ISBN 9781909031807.

Barr, Mike W, and Brian Bolland, *Camelot 3000*. London, Titan Books Ltd, 1988. ISBN 9781852860622.

BBC TV, *Doctor Who Annual 1984*. Manchester, World Distributors Ltd, 1983.

Bradley, Marion Zimmer, *The Mists of Avalon*. 1982. London, Penguin Books, 1993. ISBN 9780140177190.

Butler, David, ed, *Time and Relative Dissertations in Space: Critical Perspectives on Doctor Who*. Manchester, Manchester University Press, 2007. ISBN 9780719076824.

Rafer, David, 'Mythic Identity in **Doctor Who**'.

Campbell, Mark, *Doctor Who*. **The Pocket Essential**. Harpenden, Pocket Essentials, 2000. ISBN 9781903047194.

Cartmel, Andrew, *Cat's Cradle: Warhead*. **Doctor Who: The New Adventures**. London, Virgin Publishing Ltd, 1992. ISBN 9780426203674.

Cartmel, Andrew, *Warlock*. **Doctor Who: The New Adventures**. London, Virgin Publishing Ltd, 1995. ISBN 9780426204336.

Cartmel, Andrew, *Atom Bomb Blues*. **Doctor Who**. London, BBC Books, 2005. ISBN 9780563486350.

Cartmel, Andrew, *Script Doctor: The Inside Story of Doctor Who 1986-89*. London, Reynolds & Hearn Ltd, 2005. ISBN 9871903111895.

Cartmel, Andrew, and Christopher Jones, *Operation Volcano*. **Doctor Who: The Seventh Doctor** volume 1. London, Titan Books Ltd, 2018. ISBN 9781785868221.

Cooray Smith, James, *The Ultimate Foe*. **The Black Archive** #14. Edinburgh, Obverse Books, 2017. ISBN 9781909031616.

DeCandido, Keith RA, ed, *The Quality of Leadership*. **Doctor Who: Short Trips**. Maidenhead, Big Finish Productions, 2008. ISBN 9781844352692.

David, Peter, 'One Fateful Knight'.

Dennis, Jonathan, *Ghost Light*. **The Black Archive** #6. Edinburgh, Obverse Books, 2016. ISBN 9781909031432.

Garner, Alan, *The Owl Service*. 1967. London, CollinsVoyager, 2002. ISBN 9780007127894.

Geoffrey of Monmouth, *The History of the Kings of Britain*. c1136. Lewis Thorpe, trans, London, Penguin Classics, 1966. ISBN 9780140441703.

Gibbons, Dave, Steve Parkhouse, Mick Austin and Steve Dillon, *The Tides of Time*. **Doctor Who**. Tunbridge Wells, Panini Publishing, 2005. ISBN 9781904159926.

Gibbons, Dave, Steve Parkhouse and Steve Moore, *Dragon's Claw*. **Doctor Who**. Tunbridge Wells, Panini Publishing, 2004. ISBN 9781904159810.

Hanks, Patrick, Kate Hardcastle and Flavia Hodges, eds, *Oxford Dictionary of First Names*. 2nd ed, Oxford, Oxford University Press, 2006. ISBN 9780198610601.

Kilburn, Matthew, *The Time Warrior*. **The Black Archive** #24. Edinburgh, Obverse Books, 2018. ISBN 9781909031753.

Lacy, Norris J, ed, *The Arthurian Encyclopedia*. New York, Peter Pedrick Books, 1987. ISBN 9780872261648.

Lancelyn Green, Roger, *King Arthur and His Knights of the Round Table*. 1953. London, Puffin Books, 1995. ISBN 9780140366709.

Lane, Andy, *All-Consuming Fire*. **Doctor Who: The New Adventures**. London, Virgin Publishing, 1994. ISBN 9780426204152.

Levene, Rebecca, *Missing Adventures*. **Bernice Summerfield**. Maidenhead, Big Finish Productions, 2007. ISBN 9781844352784.

> Aaronovitch, Ben, 'Coming Soon... Bernice Summerfield: Terra Incognita, A Novel by Ben Aaronovitch'.

Lyons, Steve, *Head Games*. **Doctor Who: The New Adventures**. London, Virgin Publishing, 1995. ISBN 9780426204541.

Malory, Thomas, *Le Morte D'Arthur*. 1485. Janet Cowen, ed, London, Penguin Classics, 1969. ISBN 9780140430431, 9780140430448.

McCormac, Una, *The Curse of Fenric*. **The Black Archive** #23. Edinburgh, Obverse Books, 2018. ISBN 9781909031746.

Newman, Kim, *Doctor Who*. **BFI TV Classics**. London, BFI Publishing, 20015. ISBN 9781844570904.

Oxford English Dictionary. Compact ed, Oxford University Press, 2008. ISBN 9780199561742.

Parkin, Lance, *The Dying Days*. **Doctor Who: The New Adventures**. London, Virgin Publishing, 1997. ISBN 9780563538318.

Parkin, Lance, and Lars Pearson, *Ahistory: An Unauthorized History of the Doctor Who Universe*. 4th edition, volume 2. Des Moines, Mad Norwegian Press, 2018. ISBN 9781935234234.

Platt, Marc, *Doctor Who: Battlefield*. **The Target Doctor Who Library** #152. London, Virgin Publishing, 1991. ISBN 9780426203506.

Platt, Marc, *Downtime*. **Doctor Who: The Missing Adventures**. London, Virgin, 1996. ISBN 9780426204626.

Stanish, Deborah, and LM Myles, eds, *Chicks Unravel Time: Women Journey through Every Season of Doctor Who*. Des Moines, Mad Norwegian Press, 2012. ISBN 9781935234128.

McCormack, Una, 'No Competition'.

Sykes, Egerton, ed, *Who's Who in Non-Classical Mythology*. 1952. Alan Kendall, rev, London, Routledge, 2002. ISBN 9780415260404.

Tennyson, Alfred Lord, *Idylls of the King*. 1859-85. JM Gray, ed, London, Penguin Classics, 1983. ISBN 9780140422535.

White, TH, *The Once and Future King*. 1958. London, Harper Collins Publishers, 1998. ISBN 9780006483014.

Withycombe, EG, ed, *The Oxford Dictionary of English Christian Names*. 3rd ed, Oxford, Oxford University Press, 1976. ISBN 9780192812131.

Wood, Tat, *1985-1979: Seasons 22 to 26, the TV Movie*. **About Time: The Unauthorized Guide to Doctor Who** #6. Des Moines, Mad Norwegian Press, 2007. ISBN 9780975944653.

Periodicals

Doctor Who Monthly / Doctor Who Magazine (DWM). Marvel UK, Panini, BBC, 1979-.

Owen, Dave, 'What If?'. DWM #255, cover date August 1997.

Owen, Dave, '27 Up'. DWM #255, cover date August 1997.

Parkhouse, Steve, and Dave Gibbons, 'The Neutron Knights'. DWM #60, cover date January 1982.

Parkhouse, Steve, and Dave Gibbons, *The Tides of Time*. DWM #61-67, cover date February to August 1982.

Pixley, Andrew, 'The DWM Archive: *Battlefield*'. DWM #317, cover date May 2002.

Doctor Who: The Complete History. Volume 45 *Silver Nemesis, The Greatest Show in the Galaxy and Battlefield*. 2015.

Television

Babylon 5. Babylonian Productions Ltd, Synthetic Worlds Ltd, 1993-1998.

Doctor Who. BBC, 1963-.

   Battlefield, 1989. DVD release, 2008.

      Special Edition. DVD extra.

Knights of God. TVS, 1987.

Film

Barnfather, Keith, and Christopher Barry, dirs, *Downtime*. Dominitemporal Services, Reeltime Pictures, Tropicana Holdings, 1995.

Boorman, John, dir, *Excalibur*. Orion Pictures, 1981.

Gilliam, Terry, and Terry Jones, dirs, *Monty Python and the Holy Grail*. Michael White Productions, National Film Trustee Company, Python (Monty) Pictures, 1975.

Audio CD

Aaronovitch, Ben, and Andrew Cartmel, *Earth Aid*. **Doctor Who: The Lost Stories** #2.6. Big Finish Productions, 2011. ISBN 9781844354931.

Cartmel, Andrew, *Crime of the Century*. **Doctor Who: The Lost Stories** #2.4. Big Finish Productions, 2011. ISBN 9781844354917.

Cartmel, Andrew, *Animal*. **Doctor Who: The Lost Stories** #2.5. Big Finish Productions, 2011. ISBN 9781844354924.

Platt, Marc, *Thin Ice*. **Doctor Who: The Lost Stories** #2.3. Big Finish Productions, 2011. ISBN 9781844354900.

Web

IMDB. https://www.imdb.com/. Accessed 17 February 2019.

'Christopher Bowen'. https://www.imdb.com/name/nm0100815/. Accessed 17 February 2019.

'Marcus Gilbert'. https://www.imdb.com/name/nm0317956/. Accessed 17 February 2019.

Oxford Doctor Who Society, *The Tides of Time* #36. 2012. https://oxforddoctorwho-tidesoftime.blog/tides-of-time-issues-online/the-tides-of-time-issue-36/. Accessed 17 February 2019.

Thier, Katrin, 'Digging Around *The Stones of Blood*'.

'Azanian People's Organisation (AZAPO)'. The Heart of Hope. https://omalley.nelsonmandela.org/omalley/cis/omalley/OMalley Web/03lv02424/04lv02730/05lv03188/06lv03192.htm. Accessed 16 April 2018.

'BBC Film Censored?' The National Archive. http://www.nationalarchives.gov.uk/education/resources/sixties-britain/bbc-film-censored/. Accessed 14 April 2019.

'Past Peacekeeping Operations'. United Nations Peacekeeping. https://peacekeeping.un.org/en/past-peacekeeping-operations. Accessed 9 April 2018.

Aaronovitch, Ben, 'Back on the Menu'. *Temporarily Significant*, 21 April 2009. http://temporarilysignificant.blogspot.com/2009/04/back-on-menu.html. Accessed 16 May 2019.

Arrhenius, Professor S, 'On the Influence of Carbonic Acid in the Air upon the Temperature of the Earth'. 1897. The SAO/NASA Astrophysics Data System. http://adsbit.harvard.edu//full/1897PASP....9...14A/0000014.000.html. Accessed 16 April 2018.

Bruce, Christopher, 'Arthurian Name Dictionary'. Celtic Twilight. http://www.zendonaldson.com/twilight/camelot/bruce_dictionary/index.htm. Accessed 16 April 2018.

Cartmel, Andrew, and Carl Rowlands, '**Doctor Who**: 50 Years of Nasty Things and Groovy Monsters'. New Left Project, 19 March 2013. http://www.newleftproject.org/index.php/site/article_comments/doctor_who_fifty_years_of_nasty_things_and_groovy_monsters. Accessed 9 April 2018.

Clute, John, and David Langford, eds, *The Encyclopedia of Science Fiction*. http://www.sf-encyclopedia.com/. Accessed 17 February 2019.

'Clarke's Laws'. http://www.sf-encyclopedia.com/entry/clarkes_laws. Accessed 17 February 2019.

'Infodump'. http://www.sf-encyclopedia.com/entry/infodump. Accessed 17 February 2019.

'Magic'. http://www.sf-encyclopedia.com/entry/magic. Accessed 17 February 2019.

Cooray Smith, James, 'Lenny Henry for Doctor Who'. *Hero Collector*, 8 February 2017. https://www.herocollector.com/en-us/Article/lenny-henry-for-doctor-who. Accessed 19 March 2018.

Grahl, John, 'Obituary: Sam Aaronovitch'. *The Independent*, 8 June 1998. Archived at https://web.archive.org/web/20100901091045/http://www.independent.co.uk/news/obituaries/obituary-sam-aaronovitch-1163687.html. Accessed 18 January 2019.

Hopkins, Nick, ''Meet Nicky Moffat, the Highest-Ranked Woman in the British Army'. *The Guardian*, 11 January 2012. https://www.theguardian.com/uk/2012/jan/11/nicky-moffat-highest-ranking-woman-army. Accessed 18 January 2019.

Horne, Mark, 'Doctor Who in War with Planet Maggie'. *The Times*, 14 February 2010. Horne, Mark, 'Doctor Who in War with Planet Maggie'. https://www.thetimes.co.uk/article/doctor-who-in-war-with-planet-maggie-g2cc9hm9sq6. Accessed 2 April 2018 (paywall).

Intergovernmental Panel on Climate Change, 'History'. http://www.ipcc.ch/organization/organization_history.shtml. Accessed 16 April 2018.

Malory, Thomas, *Le Morte D'Arthur*. Project Gutenberg. http://www.gutenberg.org/files/1251/1251-h/1251-h.htm, http://www.gutenberg.org/files/1252/1252-h/1252-h.htm. Accessed 17 February 2019.

Moore, Fiona, 'You Mean All This Time We Could Have Been Friends?'. Kaldor City. http://kaldorcity.com/features/articles/missy.html.

Nennius, *History of the Britons* (*Historia Brittonum*). Ninth century. JA Giles, trans, Project Gutenberg. https://www.gutenberg.org/files/1972/1972-h/1972-h.htm. Accessed 17 February 2019.

Roberts, Tansy Rayner, '"She Vanquished Me": **Doctor Who –** *Battlefield'*. Tansyrr.com, 25 March 2011. http://tansyrr.com/tansywp/she-vanquished-me-doctor-who-battlefield/. Accessed 3 February 2019.

Tennyson, Alfred Lord, *Idylls of the King*. Project Gutenberg. https://www.gutenberg.org/files/610/610-h/610-h.htm. Accessed 17 February 2019.

Thatcher, Margaret, 'Speech to United Nations General Assembly (Global Environment)'. Margaret Thatcher Foundation. https://www.margaretthatcher.org/document/107817. Accessed 16 April 2018.

Vermaat, Robert, 'The Name of Vortigern'. Vortigern Studies. http://www.vortigernstudies.org.uk/artwho/name.htm. Accessed 16 April 2018.

BIOGRAPHY

Philip Purser-Hallard, MA DPhil, is one of the **Black Archive** series editors. He wrote *The Black Archive #4: Dark Water / Death in Heaven* and, with Naomi Jacobs, *The Black Archive #13: Human Nature / The Family of Blood*. He also writes fiction, most recently *Sherlock Holmes: The Vanishing Man* for Titan Books. He has edited six volumes of fiction for Obverse Books, and has written four novellas and more short stories than he can easily keep track of.

His trilogy of near-future Arthurian political thrillers – *The Pendragon Protocol, The Locksley Exploit* and *Trojans* – is still in print from Snowbooks, and it would be lovely if more people bought it.

Coming soon